Guyana

WORLD BIBLIOGRAPHICAL SERIES

John J. Horton is Deputy Librarian of the University of Bradford and currently Chairman of its Academic Board of Studies in Social Sciences. He has maintained a longstanding interest in the discipline of area studies and its associated bibliographical problems, with special reference to European Studies. In particular he has published in the field of Icelandic and of Yugoslav studies, including the two relevant volumes in the World Bibliographical Series.

Ian Wallace is Professor of Modern Languages at Loughborough University of Technology. A graduate of Oxford in French and German, he also studied in Tübingen, Heidelberg and Lausanne before taking teaching posts at universities in the USA, Scotland and England. He specializes in East German affairs, especially literature and culture, on which he has published numerous articles and books. In 1979 he founded the journal *GDR Monitor*, which he continues to edit.

Hans H. Wellisch is Professor emeritus at the College of Library and Information Services, University of Maryland. He was President of the American Society of Indexers and was a member of the International Federation for Documentation. He is the author of numerous articles and several books on indexing and abstracting, and has published *The Conversion of Scripts* and *Indexing and Abstracting: an International Bibliography*. He also contributes frequently to *Journal of the American Society for Information Science, The Indexer* and other professional journals.

Ralph Lee Woodward, Jr. is Chairman of the Department of History at Tulane University, New Orleans, where he has been Professor of History since 1970. He is the author of *Central America, a Nation Divided*, 2nd ed. (1985), as well as several monographs and more than sixty scholarly articles on modern Latin America. He has also compiled volumes in the World Bibliographical Series on *Belize* (1980), *Nicaragua* (1983), and *El Salvador* (1988). Dr. Woodward edited the Central American section of the *Research Guide to Central America and the Caribbean* (1985) and is currently editor of the Central American history section of the *Handbook of Latin American Studies*.

VOLUME 96

Guyana

Frances Chambers

Compiler

CLIO PRESS

OXFORD, ENGLAND · SANTA BARBARA, CALIFORNIA
DENVER, COLORADO

British Library Cataloguing in Publication Data

Chambers, Frances, *1940–*
Guyana. – (World bibliographical series; 96)
1. Guyana – Bibliographies
I. Title II. Series
016.988′1

ISBN 1–85109–070–3

Clio Press Ltd.,
55 St. Thomas' Street,
Oxford OX1 1JG, England.

ABC-Clio Information Services,
Riviera Campus, 2040 Alameda Padre Serra,
Santa Barbara, CA 93103, USA.

Designed by Bernard Crossland.
Typeset by Columns Design and Production Services, Reading, England.
Printed and bound in Great Britain by
Billing and Sons Ltd., Worcester.

THE WORLD BIBLIOGRAPHICAL SERIES

This series, which is principally designed for the English speaker, will eventually cover every country in the world, each in a separate volume comprising annotated entries on works dealing with its history, geography, economy and politics; and with its people, their culture, customs, religion and social organization. Attention will also be paid to current living conditions – housing, education, newspapers, clothing, etc. – that are all too often ignored in standard bibliographies; and to those particular aspects relevant to individual countries. Each volume seeks to achieve, by use of careful selectivity and critical assessment of the literature, an expression of the country and an appreciation of its nature and national aspirations, to guide the reader towards an understanding of its importance. The keynote of the series is to provide, in a uniform format, an interpretation of each country that will express its culture, its place in the world, and the qualities and background that make it unique. The views expressed in individual volumes, however, are not necessarily those of the publisher.

VOLUMES IN THE SERIES

1 *Yugoslavia*, John J. Horton
2 *Lebanon*, Shereen Khairallah
3 *Lesotho*, Shelagh M. Willet and David Ambrose
4 *Rhodesia/Zimbabwe*, Oliver B. Pollack and Karen Pollack
5 *Saudi Arabia*, Frank A. Clements
6 *USSR*, Anthony Thompson
7 *South Africa*, Reuben Musiker
8 *Malawi*, Robert B. Boeder
9 *Guatemala*, Woodman B. Franklin
11 *Uganda*, Robert L. Collison
12 *Malaysia*, Ian Brown and Rajeswary Ampalavanar
13 *France*, Frances Chambers
14 *Panama*, Eleanor DeSelms Langstaff
15 *Hungary*, Thomas Kabdebo
16 *USA*, Sheila R. Herstein and Naomi Robbins
17 *Greece*, Richard Clogg and Mary Jo Clogg
18 *New Zealand*, R. F. Grover
19 *Algeria*, Richard I. Lawless
20 *Sri Lanka*, Vijaya Samaraweera
21 *Belize*, Ralph Lee Woodward, Jr.
23 *Luxembourg*, Carlo Hury and Jul Christophory
24 *Swaziland*, Balam Nyeko
25 *Kenya*, Robert L. Collison
26 *India*, Brijen K. Gupta and Datta S. Kharbas
27 *Turkey*, Merel Güçlü
28 *Cyprus*, P. M. Kitromilides and M. L. Evriviades
29 *Oman*, Frank A. Clements
31 *Finland*, J. E. O. Screen
32 *Poland*, Richard C. Lewański
33 *Tunisia*, Allan M. Findlay, Anne M. Findlay and Richard I. Lawless
34 *Scotland*, Eric G. Grant
35 *China*, Peter Cheng
36 *Qatar*, P. T. H. Unwin
37 *Iceland*, John J. Horton
39 *Haiti*, Frances Chambers
40 *Sudan*, M. W. Daly
41 *Vatican City State*, Michael J. Walsh
42 *Iraq*, A. J. Abdulrahman
43 *United Arab Emirates*, Frank A. Clements
44 *Nicaragua*, Ralph Lee Woodward, Jr.
45 *Jamaica*, K. E. Ingram
46 *Australia*, I. Kepars

47 *Morocco*, Anne M. Findlay, Allan M. Findlay and Richard I. Lawless
48 *Mexico*, Naomi Robbins
49 *Bahrain*, P. T. H. Unwin
50 *The Yemens*, G. Rex Smith
51 *Zambia*, Anne M. Bliss and J. A. Rigg
52 *Puerto Rico*, Elena E. Cevallos
53 *Namibia*, Stanley Schoeman and Elna Schoeman
54 *Tanzania*, Colin Darch
55 *Jordan*, Ian J. Seccombe
56 *Kuwait*, Frank A. Clements
57 *Brazil*, Solena V. Bryant
58 *Israel*, Esther M. Snyder (preliminary compilation E. Kreiner)
59 *Romania*, Andrea Deletant and Dennis Deletant
60 *Spain*, Graham J. Shields
61 *Atlantic Ocean*, H. G. R. King
63 *Cameroon*, Mark W. DeLancey and Peter J. Schraeder
64 *Malta*, John Richard Thackrah
65 *Thailand*, Michael Watts
66 *Austria*, Denys Salt with the assistance of Arthur Farrand Radley
67 *Norway*, Leland B. Sather
68 *Czechoslovakia*, David Short
69 *Irish Republic*, Michael Owen Shannon
70 *Pacific Basin and Oceania*, Gerald W. Fry and Rufino Mauricio
71 *Portugal*, P. T. H. Unwin
72 *West Germany*, Donald S. Detwiler and Ilse E. Detwiler
73 *Syria*, Ian J. Seccombe
74 *Trinidad and Tobago*, Frances Chambers
76 *Barbados*, Robert B. Potter and Graham M. S. Dann
77 *East Germany*, Ian Wallace
78 *Mozambique*, Colin Darch
79 *Libya*, Richard I. Lawless
80 *Sweden*, Leland B. Sather and Alan Swanson
81 *Iran*, Reza Navabpour
82 *Dominica*, Robert A. Myers
83 *Denmark*, Kenneth E. Miller
84 *Paraguay*, R. Andrew Nickson
85 *Indian Ocean*, Julia J. Gotthold with the assistance of Donald W. Gotthold
86 *Egypt*, Ragai, N. Makar
87 *Gibraltar*, Graham J. Shields
88 *The Netherlands*, Peter King and Michael Wintle
89 *Bolivia*, Gertrude M. Yeager
90 *Papua New Guinea*, Fraiser McConnell
91 *The Gambia*, David P. Gamble
92 *Somalia*, Mark W. DeLancey, Sheila L. Elliott, December Green, Kenneth J. Menkhaus, Mohammad Haji Moqtar, Peter J. Schraeder
93 *Brunei*, Sylvia C. Engelen Krausse, Gerald H. Krausse
94 *Albania*, William B. Bland
95 *Singapore*, Stella R. Quah, Jon S. T. Quah
96 *Guyana*, Frances Chambers
97 *Chile*, Harold Blakemore
98 *El Salvador*, Ralph Lee Woodward, Jr.

For my Mother and Father

Contents

Introduction

Guyana is a country on the northeast coast of South America, bounded on the north by the Atlantic ocean, on the east by Suriname, on the west by Venezuela and Brazil, and on the south by Brazil. Guyana comprises 83,000 square miles of tropical rain forest, savanna grasslands and a coastal plain; the thinly-inhabited forest area accounts for nearly eighty-five per cent of the country and the coastal plain, the most populous part, for four per cent. The country's most impressive physical features are found deep in its interior: the spectacular Kaieteur Falls, a 300-foot wide 741-foot drop on the Potaro River in western Guyana, and the 9,094 foot high plateau-mountain, Mount Roraima, set on the Venezuela-Brazil-Guyana border. Jaguars, capybaras (the world's largest rodent), and tapirs are just a few of the unusual forms of wildlife found in Guyana's jungle.

The Guiana coast was sighted by Columbus on his third voyage, but not until the late sixteenth century did exploration of the region, by the Dutch and the British, begin. This period immediately calls to mind Sir Walter Raleigh, and his book, *The Discoverie of the Large, Rich and Beautiful Empyre of Guiana, with a Relation of the Great and Golden Citie Of Manoa (Which the Spanish Call El Dorado)*. Raleigh, although he probably never set foot on the territory that is today's Guyana, was responsible for linking the country with the name and the myth that are still associated with it: El Dorado, the elusive golden city of the Amerindians, said to rival Peru and Mexico in splendour, and to be lying somewhere in the jungle, always just out of reach.

In the seventeenth century, several attempts by the British to found colonies in the Guiana region proved abortive, and it was the Dutch who settled the territory known as 'The Wild Coast'. Organizing the colonies of Demerara, Berbice and Essequibo, the Dutch controlled the territory during the eighteenth century. It was during this century that a large number of black Africans were imported as slaves for the plantations, and it was during the period of Dutch rule that the most serious slave uprising in the Caribbean area occurred in Guyana: the massive Berbice Revolt which, in 1763, devastated that colony.

In the Napoleonic era, the territory changed between British and Dutch hands several times, and even became, for a short period of time, a French possession. By 1803, however, the British were securely in control and Guyana's status as a British colony was made final at the Congress of Vienna in 1814. In 1831, the three former Dutch colonies were integrated into a single political unit: British Guiana.

The nineteenth century saw Guyana boom as a sugar producer, resulting in fortunes being made in Britain. The inhuman conditions under which the slaves laboured on the plantations, however, were often criticized by British abolitionists. Events stemming from a slave revolt in Demerara, in 1823, provided the British anti-slavery movement with a martyr in the Rev. John Smith, sentenced to death for his supposed part in the uprising.

When emancipation was finally achieved, in 1834, the former slaves left the plantations, and it became necessary to find a new source of plantation labour. The planters looked to India for manpower and the indenture system under which East Indian workers were brought to Guyana was instituted in 1838, continuing until 1917. Today, the descendants of the African slaves and the East Indian indentured labourers account for the bulk of Guyana's population.

The nineteenth century was further marked by a number of events: the colony's boundaries were surveyed and set by Sir Robert Schomburgk; gold and diamonds were discovered; and, in 1899, a long-standing boundary dispute with Venezuela was thought to have been finally settled by arbitration.

Long before the twentieth century it had become evident that change was needed in Guyana, which had been left a backwater in Britain's imperial system following the decline of the sugar industry. Calls for reform became more pronounced as the twentieth century progressed and culminated, in the 1950s and 1960s, in an independence movement that for a time united Afro-Guyanese and Indo-Guyanese. However, the clash of ideologies, ethnic animosities and foreign manipulation brought turbulence and violence to Guyana, resulting temporarily in the suspension of the nation's constitution. Independence negotiations were finally successful and Guyana became an independent country in May, 1966. In 1970, the country adopted a new status as a

Co-operative Republic, and, in 1980, a new constitution was promulgated which greatly increased the power of the nation's executive. For most of Guyana's independent years its President was Forbes Burnham, the leader of the People's National Congress Party. With Burnham's death in August, 1985, Desmond Hoyte became President.

Guyana's course as an independent nation has been far from smooth and the country has continued to be shaken by disturbing events. In 1978 the Jonestown mass suicide-murders occurred, and in 1980 Walter Rodney, an outspoken opponent of the government, was assassinated. In the last ten years, the country has been beset with economic problems, and the old dispute over the country's western boundary has been revived by Venezuela, which claims 53,000 sq. miles, five-eighths, of Guyanese territory.

The aim of this bibliography is to provide a selective list of published literature on Guyana that will lead the general reader, the student and the librarian to information on the nation. The 606 entries are arranged in thirty-seven main categories. My intention throughout has been to provide a balanced picture of Guyana, which impresses one as a vivid country in which many strong personalities have worked out their destinies, more often in clashes with one other than by peaceful means. The annotations are intended to be informative and to place the works in relation to each other. In the historical categories, entries are arranged chronologically; in the other categories, the most recent items will be found first. Both books and journal articles are listed, along with a few government publications. Theses and dissertations have not been included. The final chapter lists bibliographies that cover Guyana in general, or that have been judged to be of interest to those studying more than one aspect of the country. Bibliographies of more limited subject scope have been included in the pertinent topical sections.

My thanks go to all those who have aided me in the completion of this book. Most of the material was reviewed at libraries in New York City and in Los Angeles, particularly at the libraries of New York University, Columbia University, the University of California at Los Angeles and the libraries of the City University of New York.

Once again, I wish especially to thank Stephen Chambers for his invaluable aid in this project.

The Country and Its People

1 **Guyana.**

In: *Encyclopedia of the third world.* George Thomas Kurian. New York; Oxford: Facts on File, 1987, 3rd ed. vol. 2, p. 812-28. map. bibliog.

This article presents factual information on Guyana as of 1985. Organized by topic, with highlights in 'sidebars' for quick retrieval, it includes a chart of the organization of the Guyanese government and a chronology from 1970.

2 **Background notes: Guyana.**

Washington, DC: United States Department of State, Bureau of Public Affairs, 1985. 8p. maps. bibliog. (Department of State Publication, 8095. Background Notes Series).

The most recent update (January, 1985) of a periodically revised United States government publication profiling Guyana's people, geography, history, government, political conditions, economy and foreign relations.

3 **Latin America and Caribbean contemporary record.**

Edited by Jack W. Hopkins. New York; London: Holmes & Meier, 1983- . maps. bibliog. annual.

An expertly-prepared, single-volume annual survey, that offers thematic essays on topics of special interest as well as reviews of the year's developments in political, social, economic and foreign affairs for each country of the region. The first volume was published in 1983 and covered 1981-1982.

4 **Guyana outback a lure to miners and Venezuela.**
Richard J. Meislin. *New York Times* (28 Sept. 1982), p. 2.

This newspaper report from Kaieteur Falls captures the feeling of the Guyanese hinterland and provides a summary of the basis of Venezuela's claim to five-eighths of Guyana's territory.

5 **A portrait of Guyana.**
Georgetown: Guyana Information Services, 1976. 128p.

A visual presentation of Guyana, consisting chiefly of coloured illustrations, produced by the Guyana Information Services on the occasion of the tenth anniversary of the country's independence.

6 **Guyana in pictures.**
Charles F. Gritzner. New York: Sterling; London: Ward Lock, 1975. 64p. map. (Visual Geography Series).

This illustrated introduction to the geography, history, government, social life and economy of Guyana is suitable for schoolchildren.

7 **Guyana.**
Allan Carpenter, Tom Balow. Consulting editors Samuel A. Small, T. Payne. Chicago: Children's Press, 1970. 95p. maps. (Enchantment of South America).

Attractively illustrated with photographs, this volume informatively introduces young people to the geography, history, ethnic groups, flora and fauna and tourist attractions of Guyana.

8 **Area handbook foı Guyana.**
Johnson Research Associates. Washington, DC: US Government Printing Office, 1969. Reprinted, 1980. 378p. map. bibliog.

Prepared under the auspices of the Foreign Area Studies of the American University, this compilation of factual data on the social, economic, political, and military aspects of Guyana is in need of revision but may prove useful for background information on the country's geography, history and social conditions.

9 **Guyana: a composite monograph.**
Edited by Brian Irving. Hato Rey, Puerto Rico: Interamerican University Press, 1972. 87p. map.

This collection of scholarly articles, focusing on problems confronting Guyana in the early post-independence period of the 1970s, includes the following: Brian Irving's, 'A Brief History'; Harold A. Lutchman's, 'A Review of Recent Political Developments'; Brian Wearing's, 'Present Political Situation'; Yereth Knowles's, 'Black Power'; Ved P. Duggal's, 'Economic Development Since Independence'; Della Walker's, 'Problems in Amerindian Acculturation' and Alexander D. Acholonu's, 'Wildlife and Pollution'.

10 **Co-operative Republic: Guyana 1970; a study of aspects of our way of life.**
Edited by Lloyd Searwar. Georgetown: Guyana Lithographic, 1970. 285p. bibliog.

A government-sponsored collection of essays, written at the time of Guyana's transition to Co-operative Republic status. Since many of the contributors to this book are government officials, the reader is given insight into the vision of Guyana's future as a Co-operative Republic shared by members of the ruling People's National Congress party. Social, political and economic issues are discussed, and the volume also includes articles on the Venezuela and Suriname border disputes and Guyanese culture and architecture.

11 **British Guiana.**
Raymond T. Smith. London; New York: Oxford University Press, 1962. 218p. map. bibliog.

A solid presentation of Guyana by a professional sociologist who did extensive field work in the country. Smith begins with chapters on the nation's natural resources and on its history under Dutch and British rule. He then describes the colony's economy, social structure, government and politics, as they were shortly before independence.

12 **Roth's pepper-pot, comprised of bits and pieces, odds and ends of Guianese zoological, historical and general interest.**
Vincent Roth. Georgetown: Daily Chronicle, 1958. 227p.

Although he was born in Tasmania, Roth came to Guyana in 1907 and spent his life there as a naturalist, folklorist, editor, museum curator and storyteller. In this miscellanea he brings together notes on a variety of Guyanese subjects.

13 **British Guiana; the land of six peoples.**
Michael Swan. London: HM Stationery Office, 1957. 235p. maps. bibliog. (Corona Library).

Although this book is outdated, it still contains some interesting information on Guyana and the ethnic groups that constitute its population, East Indian, African, European, Chinese, Amerindian and mixed.

Geography

14 **The West Indies; a geography of the West Indies, with special reference to the Commonwealth islands, and the mainland Commonwealth countries of Guyana and Belize.**
F.C. Evans. London: Cambridge University Press; Trinidad: Columbus, 1973. 128p. maps.

A concise presentation of basic geographical information, organized for the student and teacher, with exercises following sections of text. After the introductory chapters on general topics, such as physical geography, economic background and human geography, each country is covered individually. 'Guyana' p. 9-100, covers coastlands, forests, savannas, Georgetown and communications. The text is accompanied by maps and aerial photographs.

15 **Nelson's West Indian geography: a new study of the Commonwealth and Guyana.**
W. Williams-Bailey, P.H. Pemberton. London: Nelson, 1972. 164p. maps.

A topical geography, focusing on economic conditions in the English-speaking Caribbean.

16 **Land and people in Guyana.**
K. F. S. King. Oxford: Commonwealth Forestry Institute, University of Oxford, 1968. 150p. map. bibliog. (Institute Paper, no. 39).

A geography emphasizing land use and population distribution.

17 **Geography of Guyana.**
Leslie P. Cummings. London: Collins, 1965. 64p. maps.

This book provides a brief summary of geographical facts.

18 **The physical geography of the lower coastal plain of the Guiana coast.**
John H. Vann. Baton Rouge, Louisiana: Dept. of Geography and Anthropology, Louisiana State University, 1959. 911p. bibliog.

A technical report sponsored by the Geography Branch of the Office of Naval Research, Washington, DC, that describes the physical geography of the coastal region of the three Guianas.

19 **The interior of British Guiana and the myth of El Dorado.**
Theo L. Hills. *Canadian Geographer*, vol. 5, no. 2 (summer 1961), p. 30-43. map. bibliog.

The author of this article seeks to lay to rest the modern version of the El Dorado myth, that the Guyanese interior is a treasurehouse of unexploited rich soil and forest resources, with the potential for supporting a considerable population. Hills discusses several settlement schemes broached by the British government for the savannas of the Rupununi District, then describes the physical geography, climate and vegetation of the area, as well as its main economic activity of cattle ranching. He concludes that prospects for any sort of increased settlement in the area are limited.

20 **Recent land developments in coastal British Guiana.**
Gordon C. Merrill. *Canadian Geographer*, vol. 5, no. 2 (summer 1961), p. 24-29. bibliog.

Man's ingenuity and labour has created highly-productive agricultural land in coastal Guyana, but a formidable effort is required to maintain the drainage and irrigation works necessary to defend the low-lying lands from the sea. Merrill discusses this problem as well as describing new land development projects on the Corentyne Coast and the Canje River.

21 **Population contrasts inthe Guianas.**
David Lowenthal. *Geographical Review*, vol. 50, no. 1 (Jan. 1960), p. 41-58. maps.

In this well-documented article, Lowenthal contrasts the populations, rural settlement patterns and ethnic and cultural composition of the contiguous South American territories settled by the British, French and Dutch, in order to 'throw light on the nature and development of colonial settlement, culture, and society in general.'

22 **An investigation of the prospect for white settlement in British Guiana.**
Desmond Holdridge. *Geographical Review*, vol. 29, no. 4 (Oct. 1939), p. 622-42. maps.

The findings of an Anglo-American Commission that was sent to Guyana on the eve of the Second World War to study 'the suitability and practicability of large-scale colonization in Guyana for involuntary emigrants of European origin' are reported in this work. The commission explored the Kanaku Mountains, the Rupununi savannas, and the Marudi Mountain area to sample soil and examine vegetation. Holdridge assessed natural conditions as suitable for the proposed settlements.

Maps, Atlases and Gazetteers

23 **Atlas for Guyana and Trinidad and Tobago.**
Edited by Ada Akai, Joyce Matadeen. London: Macmillan Education, 1982. 32p. maps.

An atlas which was originally published in 1970. The 1982 edition is reprinted with revisions.

24 **Atlas of the Caribbean Basin.**
Harry F. Young. Edited by Colleen Sussman. *Department of State Bulletin*, vol. 82, no. 2066 (Sept. 1982), n.p. maps.

A special insert of thirteen unnumbered pages of maps and charts illustrates important strategic and economic features of the Caribbean Basin. The maps are limited to the countries which, like Guyana, were included in the Reagan Administration's Caribbean Basin Initiative. They show political alignments; military balance; membership of international economic organizations; agricultural growth; agricultural exports; manufacturing, refining and mining exports; export markets; import sources; energy; access to potable water; literacy and immigration to the United States.

25 **Guyana: official standard names approved by the United States Board on Geographic Names.**
Defense Mapping Agency Topographic Center. Washington, DC: US Board on Geographic Names, 1976. 123p. map. (Official Standard Names Gazetteer).

An authoritative gazetteer prepared by an American govenment agency, the US Board on Geographic Names. For each geographical name listed, the following information is provided: approved and unapproved variants, type of place or feature, latitude and longitude, Universal Transverse Mercator Grid Reference and JOG Sheet number.

26 **Guyana.**
US Central Intelligence Agency. Washington, DC: Central Intelligence Agency, 1973. Scale: 1:2,500,000.

A coloured map, showing populated places, administrative districts, railways, roads and airfields. Disputed international boundaries are indicated. It includes subject maps of economic activity, vegetation, population and ethnic groups.

27 **Gazetteer of Guyana.**
Georgetown: Cartographic Division, Lands and Survey Dept., Ministry of National Development and Agriculture, 1974. 181p. maps.

An official gazetteer, issued by an agency of the Guyanese government.

28 **Guyana.**
US Central Intelligence Agency. Washington, DC: Government Intelligence Agency, 1972. Scale: 1:3,750,000.

This is a coloured map, twenty-four by seventeen centimetres, with relief indicated by shading.

29 **Guiana and Venezuela cartography.**
P. Lee Phillips. *Annual Report of the American Historical Association for the Year 1897.* Washington, DC: Government Printing Office, 1898, p. 681-776.

A valuable bibliography, prepared by the Superintendant of Maps and Charts, Library of Congress, and utilized by the Venezuelan Boundary Commission. The main body of the work is a chronological list of maps, from 1492 to 1898, bearing on the disputed boundary question. Locations of the maps are given, and annotations are provided for some of the entries.

Geology

30 **Guyana.**
Richard B. McConnell. In: *Encyclopedia of world regional geology, part 1: western hemisphere (including Antarctica and Australia)*. Edited by Rhodes W. Fairbridge. Stroudsburg, Pennsylvania: Dowden, Hutchinson & Ross, 1975, p. 318-25. map. bibliog. (Encyclopedia of Earth Sciences, vol. 8).

Presents a concise, authoritative physical description of Guyana, with a bibliography listing many of the publications of the British Guiana Geological Survey and its successor, the Guyana Geological Survey.

31 **Guiana shield – regional review.**
Richard B. McConnell, Boris Choubert. In: *Encyclopedia of world regional geology, part 1: western hemisphere (including Antarctica and Australia)*. Edited by Rhodes W. Fairbridge. Stroudsburg, Pennsylvania: Dowden, Hutchinson & Ross, 1975, p. 309-18. map. bibliog. (Encyclopedia of Earth Sciences, vol. 8).

This gives up-to-date geological data on the Guiana Shield, the geological formation underlying the three Guianas.

32 **A new interpretation of the geology of British Guiana.**
R. B. McConnell, E. Williams, R. T. Cannon, N. J. Snelling. *Nature*, vol. 204, no. 4954 (Oct. 10, 1964), p. 115-18. maps. bibliog.

From 1957 to 1961, the Geological Survey of British Guiana carried out an intensive mapping campaign in order to prepare a new geological map of the country. This article presents a brief summary of 'the results of general interest regarding the structure and radiometric dating of the Guiana Shield and its similarities with West Africa', derived from that survey. The text is enhanced by a generalized geological map of Guyana and a stratigraphical table for the country.

33 **Geological atlas of British Guiana.**

Geological Survey of British Guiana. Georgetown: The Author, 1961-62. Scale: 1:200,000.

An authoritative geological atlas, comprising thirty sheets.

34 **British Guiana.**

S. Bracewell. In: *Handbook of South American geology; an explanation of the geologic map of South America.* Edited by William F. Jenks. New York: Geological Society of America, 1956, p. 89-98. (Geological Society of America, memoir no. 65).

A brief account that classifies and describes the rock formations of Guyana from the Early Precambrian to the Quaternary periods. The article also includes a schematic geologic section.

35 **The geology of the goldfields of British Guiana.**

J. B. Harrison. London: Dulau, 1908, 320p.

Sir John Burchmore Harrison was a government geologist who prepared a series of early reports on the country's mineral resources. This book also contains historical, geographical and other chapters by Frank Fowler and C. Wilgress Anderson, and has an appendix giving the laws and regulations governing the mining industry.

36 **Reports on the physical, descriptive, and economic geology of British Guiana.**

Charles B. Brown, J. G. Sawkins. London: Longmans, Green, for HM Stationery Office, 1875. 297p. map. (Memoirs of the Geological Survey of Great Britain).

Barrington Brown and James Sawkins were the pioneer surveyors of Guyana, completing the survey that provided the first geological data on the country.

Periodical

37 **Bulletin.**

Georgetown: Guyana Geological Survey, 1934- .

Formerly published as the *British Guiana Geological Survey Bulletin* (nos. 1 to 36), this serial publication updates information on mining and mineral resources in Guyana.

Travel Guides

38 **Birnbaum's South America 1988.**

Steve Birnbaum. Boston: Houghton Mifflin, 1987. 800p. maps. (Travel Guides Series).

Includes a four-page section giving practical information on Guyana, after first warning the reader that the country is not for the casual tourist.

39 **Fodor's South America 1988.**

New York: McKay, 1987. 640p. maps. (Fodor's Travel Guides).

Guyana is covered in the standard guide book format. There is an overview of the country, plus a 'Facts at Your Fingertips' information section.

40 **The 1988 South American handbook.**

Edited by John Brooks. Associate Editors, Joyce Candy, Ben Box. Bath, England: Trade & Travel, 1987. 1341p. maps. 64th annual ed.

This covers 'Guyana' on pages 837-49, and is the best of the travel guides for those planning a visit to Guyana. It provides valuable, detailed, up-to-date information on the country, covering both background – history, government, politics, economy – and tourist needs – hotels, restaurants, tipping, shopping, useful addresses and precautions for travel into the interior. It is especially useful for those seeking adventure in jungle areas, as current conditions are noted and exact instructions for making travel arrangements for nearly inaccessible regions are included.

41 **A cruising guide to the Caribbean and the Bahamas; including the north coast of South America, Central America, and Yucatan.**
Jerrems C. Hart, William T. Stone, Jolyon Byerley. New York: Dodd Mead, 1982. 626p. maps. bibliog. (Triton Boating Book).

This cruising handbook provides the sailor with the necessary maps, charts, diagrams and information for yachting off the Guyana coast.

42 **The pocket guide to the West Indies and British Guiana, British Honduras, Bermuda, the Spanish Main, Surinam & the Panama Canal.**
Sir Algernon Aspinall. London: Methuen, 1954. 474p. maps. bibliog. 10th ed. rev. by J. Sydney Dash. Reprinted with corrections, London: Methuen, 1960.

Aspinall's guidebook was first published in 1907 and went through many editions. Although now obviously outdated in many respects, this is one of the travel guides that continues to offer a goldmine of miscellaneous geographical, historical and architectural information. The twenty-two pages devoted to British Guiana include a map of the country and a plan of Georgetown. Aspinall calls Guyana 'a country of boundless possibilities'. For those who enjoy vintage travel information, Aspinall's book provides many entertaining facts.

Travellers' and Explorers' Accounts

43 **Travel accounts and descriptions of Latin America and the Caribbean, 1800-1920; a selected bibliography.**
Compiled by Thomas L. Welch, Myriam Figueras. Foreword by Val. T. McComie. Washington, DC: Columbus Memorial Library, Organization of American States, 1982. 293p.

An annotated listing of travel books. 'British Guiana' covers pages [51] to 54, and 'Guianas' pages [123] to 125. Criterion for inclusion in the bibliography is, 'a work [has] to be by a writer who was not a native of the area and who recorded his impressions and observations between 1800 and 1920.' Titles can all be found in the Columbus Memorial Library of the Organization of American States in Washington, DC.

44 **Climb to the lost world.**
Hamish MacInnes. London: Hodder & Stoughton, 1974, 223p. maps.

A first-person account, which describes a mountain-climbing attempt to scale the perpendicular cliff known as the 'Great Prow' and reach the summit of Mount Roraima – the site of Conan Doyle's fictional *Lost world* (q.v.). A riveting account of a British mountaineering team's successful effort to scale the impressive cliff and reach the top.

45 **Revolt in the tropics; travels in the Caribbean.**
Karl Eskelund. London: Alvin Redman, 1963. 176p. map.

The veteran Danish traveller Karl Eskelund, accompanied by his Chinese-born wife Chi-yun, travelled through the Caribbean in the early 1960s. Chapter fifteen of his book, 'Red Janet', which recounts the couple's visit to Guyana, centres on an account of leftist Janet Jagan, her husband Cheddi and their PPP government. In an interview, Cheddi Jagan explains his plans for economic reforms.

46 **The middle passage; impressions of five societies – British, French and Dutch – in the West Indies and South America.**
V. S. Naipaul. London: André Deutsch, 1962, 232p.

Literary style and aplomb characterize the seventy-six pages that novelist Naipaul devotes to his 1960 sojourn in Guyana, where he was entertained by the Jagans. He visited Georgetown, Lethem (in the Rupununi savannah country), New Amsterdam, Port Mourant, Kamarang (near Mount Roraima), and Paruima (at the Venezulan border).

47 **A hand full of diamonds, further adventures and experiences in the jungles and diamond fields of Guiana and Brazil.**
Victor G. C. Norwood. London; New York: T.V. Boardman, 1960. 235p.

This is a sequel to Norwood's *Man alone! Adventures in the jungles of British Guiana and Brazil* (London; New York: T.V. Boardman, 1956).

48 **Run softly Demerara.**
Zahra Freeth. London: Allen & Unwin, 1960. 220p.

Observations of Guyana recorded by an expatriate British woman who accompanied her husband to the bauxite mining town of Mackenzie (now known as Linden) in the late 1950s. The near four years that Mrs Freeth spent in Mackenzie produced some interesting comments on life in the colony.

49 **The marches of El Dorado; British Guiana, Brazil, Venezuela.**
Michael Swan. Boston: Beacon; London: Jonathan Cape, 1958. 304p. bibliog.

Readers will find this account of Swan's three 1955 journeys into the Guyanese interior as engrossing as any novel. Besides providing much detailed information on the country, and on Brazil and Venezuela, Swan includes sketches of many colourful colonial characters and recounts tales of the jungle. Seven informative appendixes enhance the book: 'In Search of El Dorado'; 'The Caribs'; 'A Note on the Caribs' Language'; 'Archaeology of British Guiana'; 'The Schomburgks in British Guiana' and 'Two Parallels to the Awakaipa Story of the Massacre at Roraima'.

50 **Jungle journey.**
Jo Besse McElveen Waldeck. New York: Viking, 1946, 255p.

A lighthearted description of the American author's trek through the Guyana forest, accompanying her explorer husband, Theodore J. Waldeck, in a quest for Amerindian handicrafts and implements and zoological specimens.

51 **Ninety-two days; the account of a tropical journey through British Guiana and part of Brazil.**
Evelyn Waugh. London: Duckworth, 1934. New ed. 1986, 169p. maps.

Waugh travelled through Guyana from December, 1932 to April, 1933, following an itinerary that took him from Georgetown to Boa Vista, Brazil. The trip provided him with the material for this book, an unembellished, low key but entertaining account, in which he trains his sophisticated eye on the jungle scene.

52 **Pindorama; jungle – to you!**
Desmond Holdridge. New York: Minton, Balch, 1933. 273p. maps.

A breezy, first-person account of what seems to have been a spur-of-the-moment trip to Mount Roraima with cinema equipment.

53 **Thirty years in the jungle.**
A. Hyatt Verrill. London: John Lane, The Bodley Head, 1929. 281p. map.

Chapter seven of this book, 'In the Land of El Dorado', is the first of six chapters in which Verrill describes his expeditions into the Guiana hinterland, where he studied the Amerindian tribes and collected ethnological data. His narrative is travelogue, novel, adventure story and scientific treatise rolled into one. The epitome of the intrepid explorer, Verrill, in his introduction to this book, lists some of the perils that he had to overcome in his lifelong exploration of the tropics: 'Personally I have had every tropical fever know to the medical world . . . including yellow fever, black-water fever, dengue fever, typhoid, Chagres and pernicious malaria, and I am still alive and as fit as ever.' The book has sixty illustrations and a sketch map.

54 **Jungle days.**
William Beebe. New York: Putnam, 1925. 201p.

Essays recounting the personal experiences of a naturalist in the Guyana jungle. Photographs enhance the text.

55 **Path-finding on the Mazaruni; the journal of six expeditions on the banks of the Mazaruni River in British Guiana in search of an alignment for a road or railway during the years 1922, 1923, and 1924.**
Vincent Roth. Georgetown: Daily Chronicle. 1949. 270p. map. (*Daily Chronicle*'s Guiana Edition of Reprints and Original Works Dealing With All Phases of Life in British Guiana, no. 13).

An autobiographical account of a jungle expedition by Roth, a naturalist, folklorist and editor who became curator of the British Guiana Museum. Roth's journal for the years 1918 to 1921 has also been published (*Tales of the trails*, Georgetown: Daily Chronicle, 1960).

56 **Curse of the Caribbean and the three Guianas (Gehennas).**
G. L. Morrill. Minneapolis, Minnesota: Pioneer Printers, 1920. 269p.

The Rev. Gulian Lansing Morrill was the pastor of the People's Church in Minneapolis, Minnesota. He is the author of a number of travel books in which he denounces whichever part of the world he happens to be in.

57 **Jungle peace.**
William Beebe. Foreword by Theodore Roosevelt. New York: Holt, 1934. 297p.

A personal account of the author's experiences among the inhabitants of Guyana's Bartica District, surrounded by the unspoiled flora and fauna of a tropical jungle. The book first appeared in 1918; its numerous reprintings attest to its popularity.

58 **A pioneer in Amazonia: the narrative of a journey from Manaos to Georgetown.**
William Curtis Farabee. Philadelphia, 1917. 47p. map.

Farabee was an American anthropologist and ethnologist who conducted important field studies of the South American Amerindians. This account of his pioneering jungle trek was also published in the *Bulletin of the Geographical Society of Philadelphia* (vol. 15, no. 2 (April 1917), p. 57-103).

59 **Through British Guiana to the summit of Roraima.**
Mrs Cecil Clementi (Marie Penelope Rose Eyres Clementi). London: T.F. Unwin; New York: E.P. Dutton, 1920. 236p. map.

In the winter of 1915 and 1916, Sir Cecil Clementi, Colonial Secretary in British Guiana, and his wife made an exploratory journey into a previously uncharted region of the colony's interior, mapping a route from the Kaieteur Falls on the Potaro to Mount Roraima at the Brazil-Venezuela-British Guiana border. Mrs Clementi's book describes this expedition, and is illustrated with photographs.

60 **A journey to the summit of Mount Roraima.**
Mrs Cecil Clementi (Marie Penelope Rose Eyres Clementi). *Geographical Journal*, vol. 48, no. 6 (Dec. 1916), p. 456-73. map.

A summary of the journey undertaken by the Clementis in 1915 and 1916 that was described in Mrs Clementi's *Through British Guiana to the summit of Roraima* (q.v.). This article is composed of two sections: a narrative of the journey by Mrs Clementi, followed by extracts from a lecture on the expedition delivered by Sir Cecil Clementi.

61 **British Guiana; or, work and wanderings among the Creoles and coolies, the Africans and Indians of the wild country.**
Rev. L. Crookall. London: T.F. Unwin, 1898. 247p.

The Rev. Crookall describes his travels in Guyana and the culture of its Black and East Indian population.

62 **Two years in the French West Indies.**
Lafcadio Hearn. New York: Harper & Bros., 1890. 431p. Reprinted, New York: Irvington, [n.d.]

During a voyage in the summer of 1887, Hearn's steamer touched at Georgetown, giving him the opportunity to sample Guyana's ambience. Several pages of his impressions of the town and its inhabitants are included in his essay 'A Midsummer Trip to the Tropics', which serves as an introduction to this book.

63 **Roraima and British Guiana, with a glance at Bermuda, the West Indies, and the Spanish Main.**
J. W. Bodden-Whetham. London: Hurst & Blackett, 1879. 363p. map.

The author describes his adventurous journey through the Guyana jungle to Mount Roraima in 1878. He reached the mountain but was unable to make an ascent.

64 **Canoe and camp life in British Guiana.**
C. Barrington Brown. London :E. Stamford, 1876. 400p. map.

Barrington Brown was a government surveyor who took part in the first geological survey of the Guyanese interior. He is credited with being the first European to view Kaieteur Falls, which he discovered during his explorations in 1870.

65 **The West Indies and the Spanish Main.**
Anthony Trollope. London, Chapman & Hall, 1860. 395p. map. Reprinted, London: Frank Cass, 1968. (Cass Library of West Indian Studies, no. 2).

Trollope travelled to Guyana in 1859, when the colony was Britain's largest sugar producer. He visited Georgetown, Demerara, New Amsterdam, Berbice and several sugar estates. In chapter twelve of this book, he uses the novelist's techniques of dialogue and description to present his observations, commenting on the varied races, the sugar-making process and the form of government that he found in the colony. It is in regard to the latter that he makes his oft-quoted remark, called Guyana 'a mild despotism, tempered by sugar'.

66 **Richard Schomburgk's travels in British Guiana, 1840-1844.**
Richard Schomburgk. Translated from the German and edited by Walter Roth. Georgetown: Daily Chronicle, 1922-23. 2 vols. maps.

Richard Schomburgk was a naturalist, the brother of the explorer Sir Robert Schomburgk. He accompanied his brother on several explorations of the Guyana interior, including that of October 1843, when Mount Roraima was sighted. His account of these expeditions, *Reisen in Britisch-Guiana in den jahren 1840-1844*, was published in a three-volume edition in Leipzig in 1847-48. Roth's edition of 1922-23 translates only the first two volumes; it does not translate the third volume nor the appendix of volume two. Geographical and general indexes facilitate access to the text.

67 **Robert Hermann Schomburgk's travels in Guiana and on the Orinoco during the years 1835-1839. According to his reports and communications to the Geographical Society of London.**
Robert Hermann Schomburgk. Edited by O. A. Schomburgk, with a preface by Alexander von Humboldt. Translated from the German by Walter E. Roth. Georgetown: 'Argosy', 1931. 202p.

A translation of Schomburgk's *Reisen in Guiana und am Orinoko wahrend der jahre 1835-1839*, published in Leipzig in 1841. Sir Robert Schomburgk was the principal explorer of Guyana, having been commissioned in 1834 by the Royal Geographical Society to explore the area south of the Orinoco River. He is best known for having set the western boundary known as the 'Schomburgk Line', which has since loomed large in the continuing Venezuela-Guyana boundary dispute. The reports of his explorations were published in the *Journal of the Royal Geographical Society*, beginning in 1836. This volume also contains Humboldt's *Essay on some important astronomical positions in Guiana.*

68 **Wanderings in South America, the north-west of the United States, and the Antilles, in the years 1812, 1816, 1820 and 1824 with original illustrations for the perfect preservation of birds and for cabinets of natural history.**
Charles Waterton. Edited by L. Harrison Mathews. London, New York: Oxford University Press, 1973. 230p. bibliog.

This travel classic was originally published in 1825. Waterton was an English naturalist who superintended family-owned sugar estates in Demerara. His book is organized in four parts, covering the four journeys that he made in 1812, 1816, 1820 and 1824 in South America, the northwest of the United States and the Antilles. His 1812 journey took him through 'the wilds of Demerara and Essequibo . . . to reach the Portuguese frontier-fort and collect the wourali poison'. Other journeys also led him into the Guiana jungle. His work is remarkable for its charming and detailed presentation of natural history and has been reprinted many times. The edition cited here is a modern scholarly edition which includes a short introduction, a chronology of Waterton's life and explanatory notes. A review of the book by Sidney Smith which appeared in the *Edinburgh Review* (vol. 43 (1826)) is also included.

69 **A soldier's sojourn in British Guiana, 1806-1808.**
Thomas Staunton St.Clair. Edited by Vincent Roth. Georgetown: Daily Chronicle, 1947. 281p. (*Daily Chronicle*'s Guiana Edition of Reprints and Original Works Dealing with All Phases of Life in British Guiana, no. 9).

This volume contains selections from St Clair's 1834 two-volume *A residence in the West Indies and America, with a narrative of the expedition to the Island of Walcheren.* This book was also published under the title *A soldier's recollections of the West Indies and America; with a narrative of the expedition to the Island of Walcheren.* St Clair was a British officer stationed in Demerara from 1805 to 1808.

Flora and Fauna

General

70 **Jungle cowboy.**
Stanley E. Brock. London: Hale; New York: Taplinger, 1972. 190p.

A narrative of wild animal collecting in the Guyana tropical forest which also describes ranch life on the savannas.

71 **Three singles to Adventure.**
Gerald Durrell. London: Hart-Davis, 1958; Penguin, 1964. 218p. (Adventure Library, no. 5).

An informal account by zoologist Gerald Durrell of his specimen-collecting expedition into the Guyana jungle, where he captured more than 500 examples of exotic wildlife, ranging from anacondas and anteaters to squirrel monkeys. The 'Adventure' of the title refers to the town of Adventure. The American edition of this book is called *Three tickets to Adventure*.

72 **Studies on the fauna of Suriname and other Guyanas.**
The Hague: M. Hijhoff, 1957- . (Uitgaven Natuurwetenschappelijke Studiokring voor Suriname en de Nederlandse Antillen. Uitgaven).

A multi-volume treatise on the zoology of the Guiana region, including studies of the fauna of Guyana.

73 **Zoo quest to Guiana.**
David Attenborough. London: Lutterworth, 1956; New York: Thomas V. Crowell, 1957. 185p.

A nicely illustrated book describing Attenborough's travels in Guyana in search of zoological specimens. Although this edition is out of print, an abridged version is available in paperback, entitled *The zoo quest expeditions: travels in Guyana, Indonesia & Paraguay* (Harmondsworth, England; New York: Penguin, 1980. Abridged combined ed. 355p. maps).

74 **Notes and observations on animal life in British Guiana, 1907-1941; a popular guide to colonial mammalia.**
Vincent Roth. Georgetown: Daily Chronicle, 1941. 164p. (*Daily Chronicle*'s Guiana Edition of Reprints and Original Works Dealing With All Phases of Life In British Guiana, no. 3).

This guide has fifty-four illustrations, from photographs and drawings by the author.

75 **British Guiana papers; scientific results of the Oxford University expedition to British Guiana in 1929.**
Edited by Charles Elton. London: Oxford University Press, for the Oxford University Exploration Club, 1938. 630p. maps. bibliog.

Reprints articles, brought together from various periodicals, reporting the results of the 1929 Oxford University Exploration Club expedition into the Guyana jungle.

76 **A naturalist in the Guiana forest.**
R. W. G. Hingston. London: E. Arnold; New York: Longman's Green, 1932. 384p. map.

An illustrated work, emphasizing the entomology of the tropical forest, in particular its spiders.

77 **Tropical wild life in British Guiana; zoological contributions from the tropical research station of the New York Zoological Society.**
William Beebe, G. Inness Hartley, Paul Howes, with an introduction by Colonel Theodore Roosevelt. New York: New York Zoological Society, 1917. 504p. maps.

Observations of Guyanese fauna made at the New York Zoological Society's research station at Kartabo, by Dr Beebe and his associates.

Plants

78 **The vegetation of British Guiana; a preliminary review.**
D. B. Fanshawe. Oxford: Imperial Forestry Institute, University of Oxford, 1952. 96p. maps. bibliog.

A short summary of Guyana's botany is offered in this book.

79 **In the Guiana forest: studies of nature in relation to the struggle for life.**
James Rodway. Chicago: McClung, 1912. New, rev. & enlarged ed. 326p. Reprinted, Westport, Connecticut: Creenwood, n.d. 242p.

A work on the biology of Guyana's tropical jungle that was first published in 1894 and went through numerous editions. The Greenwood Press edition currently in print is a reprint of the first edition and includes a twenty-three-page introduction by Grant Allen, a nineteenth-century writer of popular works on evolution.

Birds

80 **The behavior and ecology of hermit hummingbirds in the Kanaku Mountains, Guyana.**
Barbara K. Snow. *Wilson Bulletin*, vol. 85, no. 2 (June 1973), p. 163-77. bibliog.

This description of the behaviour of four species of hermit hummingbirds – the Pale-tailed Barbthroat, the Hairy Hermit, the Long-tailed Hermit, and the Reddish Hermit – is based on observations made between January and April 1970, in the tropical forest in southern Guyana.

81 **The birds of Guyana (formerly British Guiana).**
Dorothy E. Snyder. Salem, Massachusetts: Peabody Museum, 1966. 308p. maps. bibliog.

A check list of 720 species which contains brief descriptions, voice and distribution.

82 **The birds of British Guiana, based on the collection of Frederick Vavasour McConnell.**
Charles Chubb. London: B. Quaritch, 1916. 2 vols. map. bibliog.

These volumes, published in a limited edition of 250 copies after McConnell's death, contain a lengthy preface by Mrs McConnell.

83 **Our search for a wilderness; an account of two ornithological expeditions to Venezuela and to British Guiana.**
Mary Blair Beebe, William Beebe. New York: Holt, 1910. 408p. map.

In the Guyana segment of the journey described in this book, Dr Beebe, the American ornithologist, and his first wife travelled to the lower Barama River area where they sighted and photographed the region's avifauna.

Marine life

84 **In search of mermaids: the manatees of Guiana.**
Colin Bertram. London: P Davies, 1963; New York: T.Y. Crowell, 1964. 183p. bibliog.

Bertram's book provides interesting information on Guyana's dugongs, manatees and sea cows, creatures once mistaken for mermaids but now facing extinction. Protective legislation is included in an appendix.

85 **Notes and observations on fish life in British Guiana, 1907-1943; a popular guide to colonial fishes.**
Vincent Roth. Georgetown: Daily Chronicle, 1943. 282p. (*Daily Chronicle*'s Guiana Edition of Reprints and Original Works Dealing With All Phases of Life in British Guiana, no. 8).

An illustrated work, with an appendix, 'The fisheries of British Guiana', a report to the Comptroller for Development and Welfare in the West Indies by the Director of Fisheries Investigation, H. H. Brown. The volume also contains a glossary and a gazetteer.

Environment and Natural Resources

86 **The ecology of Guyana; a bibliography of environmental resources.**
Fred Strum, Robert J. Goodland. Monticello, Illinois: Vance Bibliographies, 1978. 44p. (Public Administration Series: Bibliography, p-61).

A list of items pertaining to the natural history, ecology and natural resources of Guyana.

87 **Handbook of natural resources of British Guiana.**
Compiled under the direction of the Interior Development Committee of British Guiana and its chairman, Vincent Roth. Georgetown: Daily Chronicle, 1946. 243p.

A comprehensive handbook with a separate, eleven-page index compiled by Vincent Roth.

Guyana: a composite monograph.
See item no. 9.

British Guiana.
See item no. 11.

Prehistory and Archaeology

88 **Ancient Guyana.**
Denis Williams. Foreword by Hugh Desmond Hoyte. Georgetown: Dept. of Culture. 1985. 94p. (Edgar Mittelholzer Memorial Lecture, no. 9).

A lecture given by Denis Williams, Guyanese artist, writer and archaeologist, on the antiquities of Guyana's Amerindians.

89 **An ethnohistory of Amerindians in Guyana.**
W. Edwards, K. Gibson. *Ethnohistory*, vol. 26, no. 2 (spring 1979), p. 161-75. map. bibliog.

After presenting general demographic information about contemporary Amerindian tribes in Guyana, the authors review theories about the prehistoric migration patterns of tribal groups into the Guyana region. They then present their own account, positing that the Warrau, Arawaks and Caribs arrived in Guyana in that order. The article includes a map of present-day locations of Amerindian tribes in Guyana.

90 **Archaeological investigations in British Guiana.**
Clifford Evans, Betty J. Meggers. Washington, DC: GPO, 1960. 419p. bibliog. (Smithsonian Institution, Bureau of Ethnology, bulletin 177).

A lengthy, major archaeological report, based on field research conducted in 1952 and 1953 in Guyana's tropical forests. After an introduction and a chapter of geographical description, the body of the report is a descriptive presentation of the data – largely pottery and shards – gathered from archaeological sites. The last chapter, 'The Cultural Sequence in British Guiana: General Conclusions and Implications', discusses the authors' inferences about the prehistoric locations of Guyana's aboriginal tribes.

91 **Secondary urn burial among Akawaio of British Guiana.**
Audrey J. Butt. *Journal of the Royal Agricultural and Commercial Society of British Guiana*, vol. 37 (Sept. 1958), p. 74-88.

Butt describes a secondary urn burial discovered at Warimaba Village on the Kamarang River in Akawaio territory.

92 **Un petroglifo mixteca en la Guayana Britanica.** (A Mixtec petroglyph in British Guiana.)
Barbro Dahlgren. In: *Homenaje al Doctor Alfonso Caso*. Mexico: Neuvo Mundo, 1951, p. 127-32.

A tantalizing piece of archaeological information; Dahlgren identifies a petroglyph from the Corentyne River as a character found in the codexes of the Mixtecs of Mexico, placing the date of its inscription between 1350 and 1660 AD.

93 **British Guiana archeology to 1945.**
Cornelius Osgood. New Haven, Connecticut: Yale University Press; London: Oxford University Press, 1946. 65p. bibliog. maps. (Yale University Publications in Anthropology, no. 36).

This volume makes an important summary and collation of data on Guyanese archaeology to 1945. After a background presentation of pertinent anthropological facts, Osgood considers pre-1944 archaeological investigations, reviewing existing data on sites and specimens. He then describes his own research, undertaken in 1944. The volume contains a map of archaeological sites and an excellent bibliography, complete to 1944.

94 **An account of some recent excavations at Seba, British Guiana.**
J. E. L. Carter. *American Antiquity*, vol. 9, no. 1 (July 1943), p. 89-99. map. bibliog.

Carter reports his excavations at a previously unknown prehistoric site in Guyana. After describing the site, and the pottery and stone implements found there, he considers some tentative hypotheses to explain the use of the site and the function of the artefacts. The account is illustrated with photographs.

95 **Origin of the Tainan culture, West Indies.**
Sven Loven. Goteborg, Sweden: Elanders, 1935. 696p. map. Reprinted, New York: AMS, 1979.

A revised second edition of Loven's *Uber die Wurzein der tainischen Kultur*, a basic treatise on the Tainan culture of the West Indies. The book summarizes what was known of the islands' prehistoric Amerindians to 1935. Mention is made of archaeological finds pertaining to the Amerindians of the Guyana mainland.

96 **Indian picture writing in British Guiana.**
Charles B. Brown. London, 1873.

A reprint of an article that appeared in the *Journal of the Anthropological Institute of Great Britain and Ireland* (vol. 2, (1873), p. 245-57). It is important for its four plates showing Amerindian petroglyphs. Illustrations of rock engravings from the southern Essequibo region can also be found in William Curtis Farabee's 'Some South American petroglyphs', in: *Anthropological essays presented to William Henry Holmes in honor of his seventieth birthday, December 1, 1916, by his friends and collaborators* (Washington, DC: James William Bryan, 1916, p. 88-95).

Periodical

97 **Journal of the Walter Roth Museum of Archaeology and Anthropology.**
Georgetown: Dept. of Culture, Ministry of Education, Social Development and Culture, 1978- . semi-annual.

A scholarly journal, dealing with the antiquities and archaeology of Guyana's Amerindians.

Historiography

98 **The historiography of the British Empire-Commonwealth; trends, interpretations and resources.**
Edited by Robin Winks, with twenty-one essays by George Bennett [et al.]. Durham, North Carolina: Duke University Press, 1966. p. 344-56.

D. A. G. Waddell's essay 'The British West Indies', discusses the historiography of the Caribbean area, including Guyana. Waddell's presentation clarifies the several viewpoints adopted towards this region by historians, covering books on the general West Indies area, volumes on specific colonies and works taking a thematic approach.

99 **British historians and the West Indies.**
Eric Williams. Preface by Alan Bullock. New York: Africana Publishing, 1966. 238p. bibliog.

An important book, which offers an analysis of British historical writing on the Caribbean area by one of the region's leading intellectuals. Williams comments on Anthony Trollope's and Thomas Carlyle's remarks on Guyana.

100 **A study on the historiography of the British West Indies, to the end of the nineteenth century.**
Elsa V. Goveia. Mexico: Pan American Institute of Geography and History, 1956. 181p. bibliog. (Pan American Institute of Geography & History, publication no. 186; Historigraficas, no. 2; Pan American Institute of Geography & History, Comision de Historia, publicacion no. 78). Reprinted, Washington, DC: Howard University Press, 1980.

A first-rate critique of historical writings on the British Carribean that were composed between the seventeenth and the nineteenth centuries. Goveia points out the assumptions made by the various authors who attempted to record the history of the area and what these assumptions imply. The book covers both general histories of the region and three works on Guyana: H. Dalton's *History of British Guiana* (q.v.), J. Rodway and T. Watt's *Chronological history of the discovery and settlement of Guiana* (q.v.) and J. Rodway's *History of British Guiana* (q.v.).

History

General

101 **A short history of the Guyanese people.**
Vere T. Daly. London: Macmillan, 1975. 326p. maps. bibliog.

This recent work by a Guyanese writer and historian covers the history of Guyana to the early 1970s.

102 **The making of Guyana.**
Vere T. Daly. London: Macmillan, 1974. 218p. maps.

A chronological account of Guyanese history, designed for use as a textbook in schools. Notes and exercises follow the text.

103 **The West Indies and the Guianas.**
D. A. G. Waddell. Englewood Cliffs, New Jersey: Prentice-Hall, 1967. 149p. map. bibliog.

A synthesis of secondary sources, which is suitable for use as an undergraduate text. Waddell takes a regional approach to the history of the Caribbean, analysing 'the general historical factors that have influenced the area as a whole and (comparing) their impact on different places, rather than (giving) a systematic account of individual territories or of the possessions of each of the imperial powers'. Although the entire region is covered, fuller treatment is given to the British territories, Guyana among them. The volume's first chapter summarizes 'The West Indies Today'; subsequent chapters recount the history of the area from 'European Settlement' to 'Development and Autonomy'.

104 **Sources of West Indian history.**

F. R. Augier, Shirley C. Gordon. London: Longman, 1962. 308p.

A book 'primarily intended for use in the senior forms of secondary schools. It is not a history in itself but a collection of [extracts taken from] various accounts written about many of the events which have taken place in the West Indies.' The selections are grouped topically as follows: people of the Caribbean, economic life, government and politics, religion and education before emancipation, slavery and its abolition, emancipation and apprenticeship, social conditions since emancipation and attempts at unification, 1831 to 1958. A valuable selection of documents pertaining to Guyana is included in the volume.

105 **Centenary history and handbook of British Guiana.**

A. R. F. Webber. Georgetown: 'Argosy', 1931. 363p. map.

A history published to mark the 100th anniversary of the final union of Demerara, Essequibo and Berbice which formed British Guiana. Webber's book is a chronological presentation of the facts of Guyanese history from 1581 to 1931, and is essentially the history of notable personalities. The volume is packed with interesting information, but its lack of an index makes it somewhat difficult to use. The thirty-four page appendix by H. P. Christiani is a 'Handbook Section', providing directory information. Six water colours by R. G. Sharples are also included.

106 **The foundation and development of British Guiana.**

J. A. J. de Villiers. *Geographical Journal*, vol. 36, no. 1 (July 1911), p. 8-26. map.

An article that is a useful summary of Guyanese history, from the sixteenth century to the nineteenth. De Villiers describes Dutch settlement in the Essequibo region in the late 1500s, recounts the life of Laurens Storm van s'Gravesande and the history of seventeenth-century Guyana under his direction, and tells about the expeditions of Sir Robert Schomburgk and other nineteenth century British explorers.

107 **The story of Georgetown.**

James Rodway, with a preface by J. Graham Cruickshank. Georgetown: 'Argosy', 1920. 143p.

This history of the development of Guyana's capital is a revision of a series of articles that originally appeared the *Argosy* newspaper in 1903.

108 **History of British Guiana, from the year 1668 to the present time.**

James Rodway. Georgetown: J. Thomson, 1891-94. 3 vols.

Volume one of this work covers the years 1668 to 1781, volume two, 1782 to 1833 and volume three, 1833 to 1893. Rodway was a prolific writer on the history and natural history of British Guiana. His three-volume general work covering the history of the colony to 1893 is a presentation that, factually, has not yet been superseded. Elsa Goveia includes an extended discussion of this book in her *Historiography of the British West Indies* (q.v.), pointing out how Rodway's blend of facts with opinion makes the work ultimately unsatisfactory.

109 **Chronological history of the discovery and settlement of Guiana, 1493-1796.**
James Rodway, Thomas Watt. Georgetown: *Royal Gazette*, 1888. 2 vols.

A straightforward compilation of historical facts on all the Guianas, covering the period from the earliest explorations to the late eighteenth century.

110 **The history of British Guiana; comprising a general description of the colony; a narrative of some of the principal events from the earliest period of its discovery to the present time; together with an account of its climate, geology, staple products, and natural history.**
Henry G. Dalton, MD. London: Longman, Brown, Green & Longman, 1855. 2 vols. maps.

A history written by a British surgeon who, in his Preface, describes his work as 'a general sketch of the history of British Guiana from the earliest discovery and exploration to the present time', (c. 1850). In the first volume, Dalton provides much detailed historical information. In chapter two of the second volume he begins his description of the colony as he found it in the mid-nineteenth century. Besides describing colonial society and the country's flora and fauna, he includes the religious history of the colony, that is, missionary attempts to Christianize the Blacks and Amerindians. The work includes an appendix of documents, statistics and a list of the commanders and governors who ruled the colony for the various colonial powers – Dutch, French, and English – from 1634 to 1853.

Periodical

111 **Timehri: Journal of the Royal Agricultural and Commerical Society of British Guiana.**
Demerara: J. Thomson, 1882- . irregular.

After independence, the title of this journal was changed to *Timehri: Journal of the Guyana Museum and Zoo*. A serial devoted to publishing articles on the history and anthropology of Guyana, *Timehri* has had a long history. Among its early editors were E. F. Im Thurn and James Rodway, well-known Guyanese historians and antiquarians.

Early exploration and settlement, sixteenth and seventeenth centuries

112 **The Dutch in the Caribbean and on the Wild Coast, 1580-1680.**
Cornelis Ch. Goslinga. Assen, Netherlands: Van Gorcum, 1971. 647p. bibliog. (Anjerpublikaties, no. 12).

A comprehensive history by a Dutch scholar of the Caribbean and the Guianas up to the demise of the West India Company, which is based mainly on Dutch archival collections, primarily the documents of the Company. Thomas G. Mathews comments in a review of this book in *Caribbean Studies* (vol. 11, no. 4 (Jan. 1972), p. 121-23), that, 'Dr Goslinga has produced a monumental work which will be consulted with care and respect by many generations of Caribbean historians because it will be many years before it is superseded.'

113 **The discovery of the large, rich, and beautiful empire of Guiana, with a relation of the great and golden city of Manoa (which the Spaniards call El Dorado) etc. performed in the year 1595 with some unpublished documents relative to that country.**
Sir Walter Raleigh. Edited with notes and a biographical memoir by Sir Robert H. Schomburgk. London: Hakluyt Society, 1848. 240p. map. Reprinted, New York: B. Franklin, 1970. (Works issued by the Hakluyt Society, no. 3).

Although Raleigh never actually set foot in the territory that is today's Guyana, this account of his search for the golden city of the Amerindians in the South American jungle stirred European interest and drew subsequent explorers to the northern coast of the continent. The myth has become so closely connected with the nation that Raleigh and El Dorado have a place in Guyanese history.

114 **The loss of El Dorado; a history.**
V. S. Naipaul. New York: Penguin, 1973. 394p. maps. bibliog.

The well-known novelist centres his book on two striking episodes in the history of the Caribbean region. The first, the quest for 'El Dorado', the Indians' fabled city of gold, lying somewhere in the Guiana region of the South American mainland, is narrated in the first part of the book, in 'The Third Marquisite'. The remaining two sections of the volume concern the history of Trinidad. Throughout the whole work the lure of the elusive city of gold in the Guyana wilderness is an underlying theme.

115 **English colonies in Guiana and on the Amazon, 1604-1668.**
James A. Williamson. Oxford: Clarendon, 1923. 191p. map.

With the close of the Anglo-Spanish War in 1604 the Guiana region on the northeast coast of South America attracted the interest of English colonizers. Charles Leigh, Robert Harcourt, Sir Thomas Roe, Sir Walter Raleigh, and Captain Robert North were among those who planned and promoted colonization schemes in the region. None of the seventeenth-century English attempts to settle the region resulted in viable colonies, and after Suriname was given up to the Dutch in 1667 at the end of the Second Dutch War, the English left the region, not to return until the Napoleonic era. Williamson's volume remains the standard account of the abortive early English attempts at settlement.

116 **The Dutch in western Guiana.**
George Emundson. *English Historical Review*, vol. 16, no. LXIV (Oct. 1901), p. 640-75.

This is an extremely interesting account of Dutch settlement in Guiana in the seventeenth century. Emundson's aim in this article is to defend the account of such settlement written by Major John Scott in 1667. This was to some extent discredited by the members of the United States Commision when it was presented during the Venezuelan boundary controversy. This article first sets forth the grounds upon which credibility may be claimed for Scott's account. The major portion of the piece corroborates the account circumstantially by comparing it with documents from Dutch, Spanish and British sources. Emundson thus shows that it is highly probable that the Dutch did establish a settlement on the Essequibo in 1616, which supports the British claim in the border dispute.

117 **The Swedish legend in Guiana.**
George Emundson. *English Historical Review*, vol. 14, no. LIII (Jan. 1899), p. 71-92.

This article deals with a point of historical curiosity that was raised during the British Guiana-Venezuela boundary controversy: a reference to a possible claim by Sweden to the Barima District, one of the districts under dispute. Emundson follows the Swedish legend through Spanish, Dutch and Swedish documents and explains a possible historical source for the alleged claim.

118 **Colonising expeditions to the West Indies and Guiana, 1623-1667.**
Edited by Vincent T. Harlow. London: Hakluyt Society, 1925. 262p. maps. bibliog. (Works issued by the Hakluyt Society, second series, no. 61).

This collection of narratives was gathered from manuscripts in British libraries. The 'Guiana' section of this volume, p. 132-257, covers the relations of English adventurers and colonizers who explored the South American coast in the seventeenth century. The editor provides a lengthy introduction summarizing early British exploration in the Caribbean area.

119 **Adriaan van Berkel's travels in South America between the Berbice and Essequibo rivers and in Surinam, 1670-1689.**
Adriaan van Berkel. Translated from the Dutch and edited by Walter Edmund Roth. Georgetown: Daily Chronicle, 1941. 145p. map. (*Daily Chronicle*'s Guiana Edition of Reprints and Original Works Dealing With All Phases Of Life In British Guiana, no. 2. Edited by Vincent Roth).

Berkel's *Amerikaansche voyagien* (Amsterdam, 1695) has been called the first book to describe extensively the area of what is now Guyana. Walter Roth's translation of this work first appeared as a series of articles in Georgetown's *Daily Chronicle* during 1926 and 1927.

Dutch colonial period, eighteenth century

120 **History of the colonies, Essequibo, Demerary and Berbice: from the Dutch establishment to the present day.**
P. M. Netscher. Translated from the Dutch by Walter Edmund Roth. 'sGravenhage, Holland: Nijhoff, 1888. Reprinted, Georgetown: Daily Chronicle, 1929. 150p.

Although it does not include all the material found in the Dutch edition – the appendixes containing the detailed notes have been omitted – Roth's translation of Netscher's *Geschiedenis van de kolonien Essequebo, Demerary en Berbice van de vestiging der Nederlanders aldaar tot op onzen tijd* makes this important work accessible to the English reader. The bulk of the work covers the history of the Dutch in Guyana up to 1814, with a short sketch of the post-Dutch period to 1888.

121 **The Dutch in the Caribbean and in the Guianas, 1680-1791.**
Cornelis Ch. Goslinga. Edited by Maria J. L. van Yperen. Assen; Dover, New Hampshire: Van Gorcum, 1985. 712p. bibliog. (Anjerpublikaties, 19).

This volume, the second part of Goslinga's major study of the Dutch empire in the New World, focuses on the Second or New Dutch West India Company, founded in 1675. His approach is thematic, with chapters concentrating on central questions. All the Dutch possessions in the Guianas are dealt with. The colonies of Essequibo and Demerara receive a chapter, as does the Berbice slave rebellion. Included is an interesting chapter on the Dutch slave code, in which Dutch law pertaining to slavery is compared with the slave regulations of the other imperial powers. Appendixes provide figures on the slave trade carried on by the Dutch.

122 **Storm van s'Gravesande: the rise of British Guiana.**
Laurens Storm van s'Gravesande. Compiled by C. A. Harris, J. A. J. de Villiers. London: Hakluyt Society, 1911. 2 vols. maps. (Works issued by the Hakluyt Society . . . second series, no. 26-27). Reprinted, Nendeln, Liechtenstein: Kraus Reprint, 1967.

This work provides extracts, translated into English, from the despatches written by Laurens Storm van s'Gravesande, Secretary and Director-General in Essequibo and Demerara from 1738 to 1772, to the directors of the Zeeland

Chamber of the West India Company. The compilers provide a 189-page introduction to the volumes that sets Storm's letters in the context of his remarkable life and of events in the Dutch colony.

123 **Some problems of slave desertion in Guyana, c. 1759-1814.**
Alvin O. Thompson. Cave Hill, Barbados: Institute of Social and Economic Research (Eastern Caribbean), University of the West Indies, 1976. 67l. bibliog. (Occasional Papers. Institute of Social and Economic Research, Eastern Caribbean, University of the West Indies, no. 4).

This short paper on slavery in seventeenth-century Guyana deals with a subject on which little has been written in English.

124 **Beschryving van Guiana, of de Wilde Kust, in Zuid-America, betreffende de aardryskunde en historie des lands . . . de bezittingen der Spanjaarden, Franschen en Portugeezen en voornaamelyk de volkplantigen der Nederlanderen als Essequebo, Demerary, Berbice, Suriname . . . Waarby komt eene verhandeling over den aart en de gewoontes de neger-slaven.** (Description of Guiana or the Wild Coast in South America concerning the geography and the history of the country . . . the possessions of the Spanish, French, and Portuguese and principally of the Dutch such as Essequebo, Demerary, Suriname . . . to which is added an essay on the character and customs of the black slaves.)
Jan Jacob Hartsinck. Amsterdam: G. Tielenburg, 1770. 2 vols. maps.

Hartsinck's contemporary account of the Dutch possessions on the South American coast is often cited as the best source for the study of the 1763 Berbice slave revolt. This rebellion, led by Cuffy, now designated as Guyana's national hero, was one of the earliest and most devastating slave insurrections in the Caribbean. Although there is no English edition of Hartsinck's book, the part dealing with the Berbice revolt was translated by Walter Roth as, 'The story of the slave rebellion in Berbice, 1763', and published serially in eight parts in *Timehri: the Journal of the British Guiana Museum and Zoo of the Royal Agricultural and Commercial Society*, nos. 20-27 (Dec. 1958-Sept. 1960).

125 **Ethnic slave rebellions in the Caribbean and the Guianas.**
Monica Schuler. *Journal of Society History*, vol. 3, no. 4 (summer 1970), p. 374-85.

An article that summarizes published sources referring to slave rebellions. The massive rebellion that took place in Berbice in 1763 is mentioned. The article is illuminating with regard to the context of slave insurrections, discussing leadership factors and types of revolts. Schuler comments that, 'Slave insurrections were a usual rather than an unusual symptom of disorganization in [Caribbean] territories, which embraced several slave systems'.

126 **Letters from Guiana, extracted from 'Notes on the West Indies . . . and the coast of Guiana.'**
George Pinckard. Edited by Vincent Roth. Georgetown: Daily Chronicle, 1942. 341p. maps. (*Daily Chronicle*'s Guiana Edition of Reprints and Original Works Dealing With All Phases of Life in British Guiana, no. 5).

George Pinckard was a military physician who accompanied Sir Ralph Abercromby's expedition to the West Indies during the Anglo-French War, reaching the area in 1796. His *Notes on the West Indies* (q.v.) were originally written in 1796 to 1797 as letters to a friend at home, and were published in England in 1806. The material reprinted here pertains to the settlements captured by the British on the coast of Guiana. Pinckard was horrified by the slave society that he witnessed in Guiana and the West Indies.

127 **Notes on the West Indies, written during the expedition under the command of the late General Sir Ralph Abercromby; including observations on the island of Barbados and the settlements captured by British troops upon the coast of Guiana; likewise remarks relating to the Creoles and slaves of the western colonies and the Indians of South America; with occasional hints regarding the seasoning or yellow fever of hot climates.**
George Pinckard. London: Longman, Hurst, Rees & Orme, 1806. 3 vols. Reprinted, Westport, Connecticut: Negro Universities Press, 1970.

This is a recent photographic reprint of Pinckard's complete work.

128 **A voyage to Demerary, by Henry Bolingbroke, 1799-1806.**
Henry Bolingbroke. Edited by Vincent Roth, with a foreword by J. Graham Cruickshank. Georgetown: Daily Chronicle, 1941. 270p. (*Daily Chronicle*'s Guiana Edition of Reprints and Original Works Dealing With All Phases of Life in British Guiana, no. 1). Reprinted, 1947.

Bolingbroke was a merchant who sailed to Demerara at the end of the eighteenth century and spent a number of years there. His description of the colony was first published in London in 1807 as *A voyage to the Demerary, containing a statistical account of the settlements there and of those on the Essequebo, the Berbice, and other contiguous rivers of Guyana.*

British colonial period, nineteenth and early twentieth centuries

129 **The profitability of sugar planting in the British West Indies, 1650-1834.**

J. R. Ward. *Economic History Review*, vol. 31, no. 2 (May 1978), p. 197-213.

In this extremely interesting article, Ward addresses the question of the profitability of the pre-emancipation sugar plantation. Based on a study of a sample of plantation records, it finds that the planters were, indeed, making a profit. The records of two Demerara plantations, Success and Vreedenhoop, provide data for the study.

130 **The historical background of British Guiana's problems.**

Eric Williams. *Journal of Negro History*, vol. 30, no. 4 (Oct. 1954), p. 357-81.

Williams sees Guyanese problems as basically economic, resulting from the decline of sugar on the world market. In this article, he discusses slavery in economic terms, refuting the charge that it was emancipation that 'ruined' the economy of British Guiana. He writes, 'It was the abolition of monopoly and not of slavery, it was free trade and not free labor, that "ruined" British Guiana . . . The architect of the "ruin" was not the African free laborer but the British free trader.'

131 **A guide for the study of British Caribbean history, 1763-1834; including the abolition and emancipation movements.**

Lowell Joseph Ragatz. Washington, DC: Government Printing Office, 1932. 725p. (Annual Report of the American Historical Association, 1930, vol. 3). Reprinted, New York: Da Capo, 1970.

This bibliographical guide for the period is indispensable. It lists literature published before 1932, mainly concerning the years in the title, but in actuality going beyond these time boundaries, and covers all types of works. There are no separate sections on the three colonies that are now Guyana, but materials on these territories – Demerara, Berbice and Essequibo – can be located through the index. Entries are provided with detailed, informative and often evaluative annotations. The sections 'Religion in the Caribbean Colonies', and 'Abolition and Emancipation Literature' list materials that should be especially valuable for research on pre-emancipation Guyanese history.

132 **The unification of British Guiana.**

Rawle Farley. *Social and Economic Studies*, vol. 4, no. 2 (June 1955), p. 168-83. bibliog.

The possibility of uniting Britain's three adjacent South American territories was first mentioned when Demerara, Essequibo, and Berbice were captured from the Dutch for the first time in 1781. However, it was not until 1831 that the three were brought together into British Guiana. In this excellent article, Farley discusses the arguments for and against territorial unification that were put forward during the fifty-year period before political integration was achieved. The account is based on research from Colonial Office papers.

133 **The Dutch and British policy of Indian subsidy: a system of annual and triennial presents.**

Mary Noel Menezes. *Caribbean Studies*, vol. 13, no. 3 (Oct. 1973), p. 64-88.

When the Dutch controlled Guyana, good relations with the Amerindian tribes were maintained largely through the distribution of presents. After the colony became British, it was necessary for the new rulers to decide on a policy in regard to these tribes, particularly whether to continue to distribute gifts in return for Amerindian aid and good will. The major part of Menezes's article describes the vicissitudes of British policy *vis-à-vis* the question of gift-giving, from the time of the takeover of the colony up to the late 1830s when regular subsidies ended. The article is based on research in primary sources in both Guyana and Great Britain.

134 **The Amerindians in Guyana, 1803-73; a documentary history.**

Edited by Mary Noel Menezes. Foreword by Donald Wood. London: Cass; Totowa, New Jersey: Biblio Distribution Centre, 1979. 314p.

Menezes has selected documents from the Public Record Office, the National Archives of Guyana and the archives of various missionary societies in order to present the reader with a picture of the British government's attitude toward Guyana's Amerindian tribes.

135 **British policy towards the Amerindians in British Guiana, 1803-1873.**

Mary Noel Menezes. Oxford: Clarendon, 1977. 326p. bibliog.

The first in-depth study of nineteenth-century British policy to discuss jurisdiction over, and protection of, the Amerindians in Great Britain's only South American colony. Menezes begins with an account of the principal tribes and their relations with the Dutch in the eighteenth century, during the period of Dutch control. She examines both Dutch and British policies with regard to Indian subsidies, and explains the roles and duties of the officials who were charged with dealing with the indigenous tribes. She also covers the issues of Indian slavery and employment, as well as the part played by the missionaries in the protection, civilization and Christianization of the Indians. The documents that are relevant to the study are included in an appendix.

136 **The traffic in slaves between the British West Indian colonies, 1807-1833.**

D. Eltis. *Economic History Review*, second series, vol. 25, no. 1 (Feb. 1972), p. 55-64.

'Between 1807 and 1833 thousands of slaves were taken from the long-settled islands such as Barbados and Dominica and shipped to the newly acquired and much less developed colonies of Trinidad and Demerara.' Demerara received imports of slaves from all across the British Caribbean; almost 15,000 slaves went to Demerara and Trinidad because of the expanding demand for sugar in Britain and the unexploited soil of these two colonies. In this article on the pre-emancipation West Indian inter-island slave trade, a subject upon which little has been written, Eltis discusses the significance of this population shift.

137 **The life and labours of John Wray, pioneer missionary in British Guiana, compiled chiefly from his own MSS and diaries.**
Thomas Rain. London: J. Snow, 1892. 376p. map.

John Wray was the first missionary to the slaves of British Guiana, and spent more than thirty years in mission work in the colony. He was sent by the London Missionary Society to a Demerara plantation in 1808, where he founded the mission that was later taken over by John Smith. Information on the 1823 Demerara slave revolt can be found in this book. Rain was allowed access to previously untapped Wray family papers for use in preparing this book.

138 **Account of an insurrection of the negro slaves in the colony of Demerara, which broke out on the 18th of August 1823.**
Joshua Bryant. Georgetown: A. Stevenson, 1824. 125p.

Bryant's is a contemporary account of the 1823 Demerara slave insurrection.

139 **Proceedings of a general court martial held at the Colony House in George Town, on Monday the 13th day of October 1823, by virtue of a warrant, and in pursuance of an order of His Excellency Major-General John Murray, Lieutenant-Governor and Commander in Chief in and over the United Colony of Demerara and Essequibo &c. pp. 204. Hatchard. London, 1824.**
Edinburgh Review, vol. 40, art. 10 (March-July, 1824), p. 226-70.

A lengthy review article commenting on the Rev. Smith's court martial and subsequent death. The anonymous author first summarizes the religious condition of the West Indian slaves and the work of the London Missionary Society to bring them religious instruction. He then recounts the story of the Rev. Smith and the Demerara revolt, quoting liberally from Smith's journals and from the proceedings of his trial.

140 **Slavery's martyr: John Smith of Demerara and the Emancipation Movement, 1817-1824.**
Cecil Northcott. London: Epworth, 1976. 136p. maps. bibliog.

Smith was a Methodist missionary who was condemned to be hanged for conspiracy for his part in the 1823 Demerara slave insurrection. He died in prison while awaiting a reprieve. Northcott's modern biography of Smith places his life in the context of the anti-slavery movement in Great Britain.

141 **Smith of Demerara (martyr-teacher of the slaves).**
David Chamberlin. London: Simpkin, Marshall, Hamilton, Kent. 1923. 110p. map.

An account of the life of Rev. Smith, published on the centenary of the Demerara Revolt. Chamberlin was the editor of the publications of the London Missionary Society and thus had access to materials from the Society's archives. This volume has a preface by Sir Sidney Oliver.

142 **The Demerara martyr; memoirs of the Rev. John Smith, missionary to Demerara.**
Edwin Angel Wallbridge. Edited by Vincent Roth. Georgetown: Daily Chronicle, 1943. 312p. (*Daily Chronicle*'s Guiana Edition of Reprints and Original Works Dealing with All Phases of Life in British Guiana, no. 6).

Wallbridge's work, based on Smith's letters and journal, was first published in 1848. The 1943 edition, edited by Vincent Roth adds 'prefatory notes containing hitherto unpublished historical matter' by J. Graham Cruickshank. Wallbridge's original edition, which has a preface by the Rev. W. G. Barrett, was reprinted in 1969 (New York: Negro Universities Press, 274p.). Wallbridge was himself a missionary in Guyana. The last two chapters of his book deal with the history of the Guyanese missions after Smith's death up to the mid-1840s.

143 **The London Missionary Society's report on the proceedings against the late Rev. J. Smith of Demerara . . . who was tried under martial law and condemned to death, on a charge of aiding and assisting in a rebellion of the negro slaves.**
London Missionary Society. London: F. Westley, 1824. 204p. Reprinted, New York: Negro Universities Press, 1969.

This report of the case against the Rev. Smith for his part in the 1823 Demerara Revolt was published by the Directors of the London Missionary Society, under whose aegis Smith had gone to Demerara in 1817. The report includes documentary evidence that was omitted from the Parliamentary report of the trial, as well as an appendix containing the letters and statements of the Rev. and Mrs Smith.

144 **Testing the chains: resistance to slavery in the British West Indies.**
Michael M. Craton. Ithaca, New York: Cornell University Press, 1982. 389p. maps.

In chapter twenty-one, 'The Demerara Revolt, 1823', Craton tells the story of the August 1823 slave insurrection on East Coast, Demerara, led by Quamina, Jack Gladstone and others, who rose against 'the cruelest plantation regime in the hemisphere'. The rest of the book provides information about slavery in the British West Indies that would interest those studying the slave insurrection in Guyana.

145 **Proto-peasant revolts? The late slave rebellions in the British West Indies, 1816-1832.**

Michael M. Craton. *Past & Present*, no. 85 (Nov. 1979), p. 99-125. map.

Drawing his information from primary sources, Craton discusses the causes, nature and ends of the three late slave rebellions in the British Caribbean. The rebellions discussed occurred in Barbados, in 1816, in Demerara, in 1823 and in Jamaica, in 1831-1832. The article provides concise information on the Demerara insurrection, which began on 18 August 1823, on Le Resouvenir estate and the adjacent Success estate. It was led by Quamina, who had been the Rev. John Smith's chief deacon, and by Quamina's son, Jack.

146 **British slavery and its abolition, 1823-1838.**

William Law Mathieson. London: Longman, 1926. 318p.

This is still the standard account of the abolition of slavery by the British in their West Indian colonies, including Guyana. Mathieson's *British slave emancipation, 1838-1849* (London: Longman, Green, 1932) is a sequel to this volume. Another older history of the emancipation era that has not yet been superseded is William L. Burn's *Emancipation and apprenticeship in the British West Indies* (London: Cape, 1937).

147 **British slave emancipation; the sugar colonies and the great experiment, 1830-1865.**

William A. Green. London: Oxford University Press, 1976. 449p. maps. bibliog.

Offers the first comprehensive treatment of the effects of the emancipation of the slaves in the British colonies since William Law Mathieson's work (q.v.). Green's book is principally an examination of the Colonial Office's handling of the problem of slavery and its abolition, and traces the shifts in Britain's colonial policy regarding the post-emancipation labour force. A critical review of this book by B. W. Higman can be found in the *Journal of Economic History* (vol. 37, no. 2 (June 1977), p. 515-17).

148 **The economic impact of slave emancipation in British Guiana, 1832-1852.**

Michael Moohr. *Economic History Review*, second series, vol. 25, no. 4 (Nov. 1972), p. 588-607.

'This article is an attempt to assess the impact the abolition of slavery had on the structure of output, pattern of resource allocation and, to a lesser extent, distribution of income in British Guiana between 1832 and 1852 . . . Starting with a set of colonial national income accounts for both the pre-emancipation economy of 1832 and the post-emancipation economy of 1852, the major features of economic changes which occurred between these two decades are set out and quantified. Once this step has been completed and the question of timing settled, these changes are then related back to slavery and its abolition.' Data is presented in tabular form.

149 **The apprenticeship in British Guiana, 1834-1838.**
William A. Green. *Caribbean Studies*, vol. 9, no. 2 (July 1969), p. 44-66.

In this detailed, scholarly article, based on research in Colonial Office papers, Green examines 'the transition from a slave to a free society in the second of Britain's West Indian holdings, British Guiana, noting the distinguishing characteristics of that colony in its physical form and in the operation of its apprenticeship'.

150 **A description of British Guiana, geographical and statistical: exhibiting its resources and capabilities, together with the present and future condition and prospects of the colony.**
Robert H. Schomburgk. London: Simpkin, Marshall, 1840. Reprinted, London: Frank Cass, 1970. 155p. map. (Cass Library of West Indian Studies, no. 10).

Schomburgk describes his book as 'an account of whatever relates to the physical structure, productions and present and future capabilities of the colony of British Guiana, including the statistical information I have been able to procure'. The book is based on information gathered by Schomburgk during his expeditions in Guyana between 1835 and 1839.

151 **The Caribbean in transition: papers on social, political, and economic development.**
Edited by F. M. Andic, T. G. Mathews. Rio Piedras, Puerto Rico: Institute of Caribbean Studies, University of Puerto Rico, 1965. 353p.

K. O. Laurence's 'Evolution of long-term labour contracts in Trinidad and British Guiana, 1834-1863' can be found in this collection of papers from the second Caribbean Scholars' Conference, held at the University of the West Indies, Mona, Jamaica, in April, 1964. This essay on the development of indenture contracts was also published in the *Jamaican Historical Review*, vol. 5 (1965). Other papers found in this volume would be of interest to Caribbeanists.

152 **Sugar without slaves: the political economy of British Guiana, 1838-1904.**
Alan H. Adamson. New Haven, Connecticut; London: Yale University Press, 1972. 315p. maps. bibliog.

A social and economic history that is required reading for those wishing to understand Guyana's past and present. Adamson provides a valuable analysis of the survival of the sugar-plantation economy from the emancipation of the slaves in 1838 up to the replacement of the plantocracy by limited liability companies in 1904. He traces the evolution of the social groupings within this period: the black peasantry, the plantation labourers, the indentured immigrants and the planters. The book is based on research in Colonial Office and Public Record Office papers.

153 **The rise of the village settlements of British Guiana.**
Rawle Farley. *Caribbean Quarterly*, vol. 3, no. 2 (Sept. 1953), p. 101-9.

Villages, independent of the plantations, were first settled by runaway slaves. Farley traces the history of their development after emancipation up to the middle of the nineteenth century.

154 **Eight years in British Guiana; being a journal of a residence in that province, from 1840 to 1848, inclusive, with anecdotes and incidents illustrating the social conditions of its inhabitants; and the opinions of the writer on the state and prospects of our sugar colonies generally.**
Barton Premium (pseud.). London: Longman, Brown, Green, & Longman, 1850. 305p.

This description of social conditions in the post-emancipation era, seen from the point of view of a sugar planter, was published under a pseudonym.

155 **Experiences of a Demerara magistrate, 1863-69, with an appendix comprising the author's letter to the secretary of state for the colonies on the subject of the treatment of East Indian immigrants on sugar estates.**
Sir G. William Des Voeux. Edited with a foreword by Vincent Roth. Georgetown: Daily Chronicle, 1948. 148p. (Guiana edition, no. 11).

A primary printed source for the history of mid-nineteenth-century British colonialism in Guyana, this volume reprints the first nine chapters of its author's *My colonial service in British Guiana, St. Lucia, Trinidad, Fiji, Australia, Newfoundland, and Hong Kong, with interludes* (London: J. Murray, 1903. 2 vols). Des Voeux was a stipendary maigstrate in British Guiana from 1863 to 1869, during which time he incurred the enmity of the sugar planters for his defence of East Indian immigrants. His letter of 25 December 1869 to Lord Granville, Secretary of State for the Colonies, complaining of the conditions under which the East Indians lived and worked can be found in the appendix of this volume. This letter resulted in the appointment of a Royal Commission to investigate the colonists' practices towards their indentured labourers.

156 **Sir Francis Hincks, a study of Canadian politics, railways and finance in the nineteenth century.**
Ronald Stewart Longley. Toronto: University of Toronto Press, 1943. 480p. bibliog.

A biography of Sir Francis Hincks, who was Governor of British Guiana from 1862 to 1869. Hincks was Canadian, although a native of Ireland. His administration accommodated the planters by instituting repressive measures against their East Indian labourers. It was on account of Hincks's policies that the Royal Commission to Enquire into the Treatment of Immigrants in British Guiana was appointed in 1870.

157 **The coolie, his rights and wrongs; notes of a journey to British Guiana, with a review of the system and of the recent commission of inquiry.**

Edward Jenkins. London: Strahan, 1871. 446p. map.

Jenkins was a British barrister who went to Guyana on behalf of the Aborigines Protection and Anti-Slavery Society to report on the Royal Commission to Enquire into the Treatment of Immigrants in British Guiana. After a short visit to the colony, he published this book, in which he champions the East Indian indentured labourers.

158 **The colony of British Guiana and its labouring population: containing a short account of the colony, and brief descriptions of the black Creole, Portuguese, East Indian, and Chinese coolies . . . collected . . . from sundry articles published . . . at different times.**

H. V. P. Bronkhurst. London: T. Woolmer, 1883. 479p.

This book describes the social and working conditions of the Guyanese labouring classes in the mid-nineteenth-century colony. Bronkhurst was a Methodist missionary who went to Guyana in 1860. His book contains much on the work of the missions. He is also the author of *Among the Hindus and Creoles of British Guyana* (London: T. Woolmer, 1888), in which he describes the life and customs of the colony's East Indians and Blacks.

159 **Twenty-five years in British Guiana.**

Henry Kirke. Westport, Connecticut: Negro Universities Press, 1970. 364p.

This volume is a reprint of a book first published in 1898. Kirke was a magistrate and Sheriff of Demerara in the late-nineteenth century. His volume includes much information on the social life and customs of the time.

160 **The post-indenture experience of East Indians in Guyana, 1873-1921.**

Lesley M. Potter. In: *East Indians in the Caribbean; colonialism and the struggle for identity: papers presented to a symposium on East Indians in the Caribbean, The University of the West Indies, June, 1975*. Preface by Bridget Brereton, Winston Dookeran with an introduction by V. S. Naipaul. Millwood, New York; London; Nendeln, Liechtenstein: Kraus International, 1982, p. 71-92. maps.

A paper concerned with the behaviour of indentured East Indians after 1873. By the terms of the June 1873 Immigration Ordinance, the East Indians, after the termination of their indenture period, were allowed the choices of staying on their original estates or moving away, and of staying in Guyana or returning to India. Potter deals with the strategies adopted by the planters to regulate East Indian movements, the East Indians' migration process and the patterns that resulted from their migration choices. Maps, charts and tables clarify the information presented in the text.

161 **A history of the Guyanese working people, 1881-1905.**
Walter Rodney. Foreword by George Lamming. Baltimore, Maryland; London: Johns Hopkins University Press, 1981. 282p. bibliog. (Johns Hopkins Studies in Atlantic History and Culture).

Rodney utilizes a socio-economic approach in this history of the evolution of the Guyanese social classes, from the 1880s to the 1905 Demerara riots. Published posthumously, in 1982, this book was awarded the American Historical Society's Albert J. Beveridge award for the best book in English on the history of the United States, Canada, or Latin America published in the previous year.

162 **Guyana: the making of the labour force.**
Walter Rodney. *Race & Class*, vol. 22, no. 4 (spring 1981), p. 331-52.

A shortened version of the chapter 'The evolution of the plantation labor force in the nineteenth cnetury', from Rodney's *History of the Guyanese working people, 1881-1905* (q.v.). Rodney discusses free against indentured labour on the sugar plantations, and the planters' attempts to profit the most out of both.

163 **Guyanese sugar plantations in the late nineteenth century: a contemporary description from the 'Argosy'.**
Edited with an introduction by Walter Rodney. Georgetown: Release, 1979. 97p.

A reprint of a series of articles, 'Our sugar estates', by an anonymous reporter, first published in the *Argosy* newspaper from February to September, 1883. The articles describe sugar plantations on the Essequibo coast, in Demerara and in Berbice.

164 **Quinton Hogg: a biography.**
Ethel M. Hogg, with a preface by the Duke of Argyll. London: A. Constable, 1904. 419p.

Quinton Hogg was the senior partner in the London firm of Hogg, Curtis and Campbell, which owned sugar estates in Guyana, including Plantation Bel Air, near Georgetown, and several others. Hogg often visited these holdings.

165 **The discovery of gold and the development of peasant industries in Guyana, 1884-1914; a study in the political economy of change.**
Michael Moohr. *Caribbean Studies*, vol. 15, no. 2 (July 1975), p. 57-72.

Moohr studies the phenomenon of the sudden appearance in the late 1880s and 1890s of peasant-dominated industries in Guyana. He concludes that this puzzling development resulted from the freeing of colonial resources for non-plantation uses. This release of resources was itself caused by the emergence of the gold industry, which broke the exclusive monopoly of labour enjoyed by the sugar planters, who until then had reaped most of the benefits of the colony's plantation economy.

166 **Patronage in colonial society: a study of the former British Guiana.**
Harold A. Lutchman. *Caribbean Quarterly*, vol. 16, no. 2 (June 1970), p. 34-50.

'In this study the concern will be not so much with the question of how patronage affected the colonial civil servant as with its impact on the politician, particularly during the period between 1891 and 1928.' Lutchman sees patronage as quite common during the colonial era, and as serving a useful purpose for administrators faced with the task of governing colonial peoples. His article examines the constitutional setting for patronage in colonial Guyana, the politicians' behaviour in regard to it, the role of the governor and the function of patronage.

167 **Note on emigration from India to British Guiana.**
D. W. D. Comins. Georgetown: Baldwin, 1894. 100p.

Surgeon-Major Comins was an officer in the Indian Service, the Protector of Emigrants at Calcutta. In 1892 he was assigned to investigate the conditions under which Indians who had emigrated to various parts of the world laboured. He visited overseas colonies, including those in the Caribbean region and issued a number of reports judging the indenture system to be, generally, satisfactorily managed.

168 **The immigration issue in British Guiana, 1903-1913; the economic and constitutional origins of racist politics in Guyana.**
Peter D. Fraser. *Journal of Caribbean History*, vol. 14 (1981), p. 18-45.

'From 1903 to 1913 there was much public discussion of Indian indentured immigration in British Guiana.' In this article, Fraser shows that 'racial feeling played a minor part and that the controversies were generated by the economic problems of Guianese society and a shift in the balance of political forces'.

169 **East India (indentured labour); report to the Government of India on the conditions of Indian immigrants in four British colonies and Surinam.**
James McNeill, Chimman Lal. London: HM Stationery Office, 1915. 2 vols. (Great Britain Parliament Papers by Command, Cd. 7744, 7745).

Volume one of this work is *Trinidad and British Guiana*; volume two is *Surinam, Jamaica, Fiji and general remarks*. They comprise a report submitted to the Secretary of the Government of India Commerce and Industry Department. McNeill was a member of the Indian Civil Service appointed by the Viceroy of India, Lord Hardinge, to investigate the conditions of indentured Indian labourers. His report recommended the continuation of the indenture system, in spite of the fact that much of the evidence it contained had negative implications and could have been used equally effectively in support of the opposite conclusion.

170 **Official attitudes and official violence; the Ruimveldt Massacre, Guyana, 1924.**
Ann Spackman. *Social and Economic Studies*, vol. 22, no. 3 (Sept. 1973), p. 315-34. bibliog.

'In 1924 at Ruimveldt in British Guiana . . . thirteen people were killed and twenty-four wounded as the result of an order to shoot into a crowd of estate labourers who were marching to Georgetown. The order to shoot was given by staff officer Captain Ramsey to a combined force of armed military and police . . . This case study is concerned with the shooting of unarmed people and it seeks to show how extreme violence was chosen as a course of action, and how it was justified in the minds of officials.' Research in Colonial Office papers is the basis of this article.

171 **The rise of the first mass-based multi-racial party in Guyana.**
Ralph R. Premdas. *Caribbean Quarterly*, vol. 20, nos. 3 & 4 (Sept.–Dec. 1975), p. 5-20.

The People's Progressive Party was launched in 1950, its forerunner having been the Political Affairs Committee. Premdas unravels the political aspects of the early PPP, as it was before the formal Cheddi Jagan – Forbes Burnham leadership split in 1955. During this time the PPP was multi-racial and followed a programme that aimed at eliminating colonialism and instituting a socialist society in Guyana. After the split, Jagan and Burnham each led his own party, largely representing racial blocs.

172 **Trouble in Guyana: an account of people, personalities and politics as they were in British Guiana.**
Peter Simms. London: Allen & Unwin, 1966. 198p. map. bibliog.

This work is concerned with recent Guyanese history. After several chapters of social and historical background, Simms focuses on Cheddi and Janet Jagan, and their People's Progressive Party during the 1950s and 1960s, a time during which the Jagans and the PPP were at the centre of tumultuous political events.

173 **The party system in British Guiana and the General election of 1961.**
C. Paul Bradley. *Caribbean Studies*, vol. 1, no. 3 (Oct. 1961), p. 1-26.

A lucid analysis of the party system of Guyana, as evinced in the 1961 General Election, which gave Cheddi Jagan's People's Progressive Party a substantial victory. Bradley notes the dominance of party-oriented politics in the nation, in which the personalities of the leaders are primary, and concludes that, 'the development of a stable two-party system in British Guiana is not imminent'.

174 **The end of a colony: British Guiana, 1962.**
T. E. M. McKitterick. *Political Quarterly*, vol. 33, no. 1 (Jan.–March 1962), p. 30-40.

A snapshot of Guyanese politics and the country's relations with Great Britain and the United States on what was, supposedly, the eve of independence.

175 **The end of a colony – II.**
B. A. N. Collins. *Political Quarterly*, vol. 36, no. 4 (Oct.–Dec. 1965), p. 406-16.

A follow-up to T. E. M. McKitterick's article of 1962 (q.v.), which was written at a time when Guyanese independence was thought to be close at hand. Collins examines how and why this expectation of independence was not fulfilled, discussing the problems that prevented independence in 1962 and that still remain as another constitutional conference is scheduled to begin: 'Dr Jagan's ideology and the suspicions it arouses, animosity between the colony's principal ethnic groupings, and international strategic concerns viewed from Washington as well as [London].'

Independent Guyana, 1966- .

176 **A political and social history of Guyana, 1945-1983.**
Thomas J. Spinner, Jr. Boulder, Colorado; London: Westview, 1984. 244p. bibliog. maps.

A recent study by an American historian that concentrates on the shifting policies of post-1950s developments in Guyana. In this well-informed and well-documented account, Spinner follows the evolution of the country's politicians and political parties and charts the economic and human rights decline of the country.

177 **Guyana emergent: the post-independent struggle for nondependent development.**
Robert H. Manley. Cambridge, Massachusetts: Schenkman, 1982. Rev. ed. 176p. bibliog.

Originally published in 1979, the main text of this book covers the first ten years, 1966 to 1976, of Guyana's political independence from Great Britain. Manley discusses the political leadership within the nation, foreign relations with the Caribbean region, territorial disputes with Venezuela and Suriname, foreign relations with the rest of the world and the consolidation of the country's identity. The volume is based on first-hand research in Guyana, predominantly extensive interviews with prominent political figures. There is a 'List of Interviews' on pages 119 and 120. In the 1982 revised edition, the main body of the work remains unchanged, with the author adding a short epilogue commenting on events from 1976 to 1980, principally the Rodney assassination on 13 June 1980. The revised edition also contains a selected bibliography.

178 **Race vs. politics in Guyana: political cleavages and political mobilisation in the 1968 general election.**
J. E. Greene. Kingston, Jamaica: Institute of Social & Economic Research, University of West Indies, 1974. 198p. bibliog.

The results of a survey conducted after Guyana's first post-independence general election indicate that 'race' remains the deciding factor for the Guyanese voter.

Greene's study not only reports and discusses the results of this survey, but also clarifies the history of elections in Guyana, 1831 to 1968. The text of the volume is supplemented by many tables.

179 **Georgetown journal: a Caribbean writer's journey from London via Port of Spain to Georgetown, Guyana, 1970.**
Andrew Salkey. London: New Beacon, 1972. 416p.

Salkey, a Jamaican novelist, poet and editor, reports on social and political conditions in Guyana as the nation becomes a Co-operative Republic.

180 **Letter from Guyana.**
Jane Kramer. *New Yorker* (16 Sept. 1974), p. 100-28.

Kramer offers intelligent reporting on Guyanese politics, race relations and the country's economic situation in 1974.

181 **Guyana update: political, economic, moral bankruptcy.**
Thomas J. Spinner, Jr. *Caribbean Review*, vol. 11, no. 4 (fall 1982), p. 8-11 & 30-32.

Spinner records the economic calamities, the devastating political situation, the human rights disasters, the foreign relations crises and the deteriorating state of education, health and housing in Guyana, in the 1970s and early 1980s.

182 **Making sense of the Jonestown suicides; a sociological history of Peoples Temple.**
Judith Mary Weightman. New York; Toronto, Canada: Edwin Mellen, 1983. 220p. bibliog. (Studies in Religion and Society, vol. 7).

In this volume, the author critically examines accounts of the Jonestown disaster and of the experiences that preceded the mass suicides, in order to make an objective analysis of the Peoples Temple and its membes. It is a documented account, based on an extensive list of sources.

183 **The children of Jonestown.**
Kenneth Wooden. New York: McGraw-Hill, 1981. 238p. bibliog.

This account of the Jonestown disaster centres on the 276 children who died there. Besides being a heart-breaking account of the abuse and murder of innocent victims, this book is also an indictment of the American legal system, for its failure to protect the children of the Peoples Temple devotees.

184 **Journey to nowhere: a new world tragedy.**
Shiva Naipaul. New York: Simon & Schuster, 1981. 336p. bibliog.

Trinidadian novelist Shiva Naipaul visited Guyana and Jonestown after the mass suicide. His book on the event is a meditation on the tragedy and on the society that spawned it.

185 **Our father who art in hell.**

James Reston, Jr. New York: Times, 1981. 338p.

Reston's volume on the Jonestown tragedy focuses on the life and personality of the leader of the Peoples Temple, Jim Jones. The book is based on interviews with survivors and with relatives of the suicide victims, on tape recordings and documents obtained from the Federal Bureau of Investigation and on the records of the Peoples Temple.

186 **The cult that died; the tragedy of Jim Jones and the Peoples Temple.**

George Klineman, Sherman Butler, David Conn. New York: Putnam, 1980. 372p.

A solid exposé of the Peoples Temple cult that its authors began writing before the Guyana suicides brought the group to public notoriety. It is based on extensive interviews with Temple defectors and survivors, with research by Anthony O. Miller.

187 **The strongest poison.**

Mark Lane. New York: Hawthorn, 1980. 494p.

Radical attorney Mark Lane presents an account of the Jonestown disaster and its aftermath that contradicts news media reports. The volume includes appendixes of documents and correspondence pertaining to the tragedy.

188 **'Gather with the saints at the river': the Jonestown holocaust of 1978; a descriptive and interpretative essay on its ultimate meaning from a Caribbean viewpoint.**

Gordon K. Lewis. Rio Piedras, Puerto Rico: Institute of Caribbean Studies, University of Puerto Rico, 1979. 50p.

A Caribbean scholar here analyses the Jonestown disaster.

189 **Guyana's 1980 elections: the politics of fraud.**

Lord Avebury, British Parliamentary Human Rights Group. *Caribbean Review*, vol. 10, no. 2 (spring 1981), p. 8-11 & 44.

In this article the editors of *Caribbean Review* synthesize data from the official report of the International Observer Team on Guyana's 1980 elections, which were won by Forbes Burnham and the People's National Congress. The Observer team found evidence of massive and flagrant electoral fraud and voter intimidation.

190 **Walter Rodney: revolutionary and scholar. A tribute, proceedings of a memorial symposium held on the UCLA campus, January 30, 1981.**
Edited by Edward A. Alpers, Pierre-Michel Fontaine. Los Angeles: African Studies Centre and the Centre for Afro-American Studies, University of California, Los Angeles, 1983.
200p.

Rodney, scholar, historian, political activist and opponent of the PNC-Burnham government, was the victim of a bizarre assassination in Guyana in June, 1980. These papers were read at a memorial symposium, and include essays on his life, politics and scholarly work.

191 **The making of an organic intellectual: Walter Rodney (1942-1980).**
Trevor A. Campbell. *Latin American Perspectives*, issue 28, vol. 8, no. 1 (winter 1981), p. 49-63. bibliog.

A biography of Walter Rodney, the assassinated Guyanese political activist. Campbell emphasizes Rodney's scholarship and political involvements.

192 **Guyana: a nation in ruins; the Puerto Rican model failed; the People's National Congress, Forbes Burnham and political opportunism.**
Paul Nehru Tennassee. Toronto: Guyanese Research & Representation Services, 1982. 104p.

A Guyanese teacher and researcher severely criticizes Burnham and the People's National Congress.

193 **The Caribbean; survival, struggle and sovereignty.**
Catherine A. Sunshine. Boston, Massachusetts: South End, 1985. 232p. maps. bibliog. (EPICA Publication).

In this book, a chapter entitled 'Guyana, Pseudo-Socialism and Starvation' paints a bleak picture of the recent Burnham era in Guyanese history. The author views Burnham's socialism as 'a guise for consolidating his party's power', and describes the economic crisis that was wracked the country since the mid-1970s. An extract from the 'Interim Report of the Joint Mission to Investigate Political Freedom in Guyana, May 1985', issued by the British Parliamentary Human Rights Group and Americas Watch' is pessimistic about the nation's future as a democracy. A postscript to the chapter notes that Burnham died on 6 August 1985 and that Desmond Hoyte is now Guyana's President. The rest of the book is also of interest to those studying the situation in Guyana.

Population and Nationalities

Population and fertility, twentieth century

194 **A review of the fertility situation in countries in the region of the Economic Commission for Latin America and the Caribbean.**
Economic Commission for Latin America and the Caribbean. In: *Fertility behaviour in the context of development: evidence from the World Fertility Survey*. Edited by the United Nations Department of Economic and Social Affairs. New York: United Nations, 1987, p. 299-323. bibliog.

Guyana was among the countries that participated in the World Fertility Survey in the 1970s. This article is a report on the data gathered in that survey from the thirteen countries in the region of the Economic Commission for Latin America and the Caribbean. It provides, 'a general description of recent fertility trends in each country as well as a review of related topics (prevalence of childlessness and infecundity, strength of sex preferences and trends in infant and child mortality) and provides a backdrop for the discussion of socio-economic determinants of fertility.' The data upon which the report is based is presented in tabular form.

195 **Evaluation of the Guyana fertility survey 1975.**
Sundat Balkaran. Voorburg, Netherlands: International Statistical Institute; London: World Fertility Survey, 1982. 37p. bibliog. (Scientific Reports, no. 26, Feb. 1982).

Balkaran considers 'vital registration data for recent periods in Guyana fairly reliable', although he does detect some discrepancies between such data and figures from the World Fertility Survey. The latter data shows a higher level of fertility than the rate calcualted from Guyana's vital statistics, but both indicate a decline in the nation's fertility.

196 **Guyana fertility survey, 1975; country report.**
Statistical Bureau. Ministry of Economic Development. Georgetown: The Author, 1976. 2 vols.

A compilation of statistics on human fertility in Guyana, which was gathered as part of the United Nations–sponsored World Fertility Survey.

197 **1970 Population census of the Commonwealth Caribbean, 7 April and 25 October.**
Census Research Programme, University of the West Indies. Mona, Jamaica: Census Research Programme, 1973.

Guyana is included in this multi-volume report on the population of the Caribbean.

198 **Population and Vital Statistics Report.**
Georgetown: Statistical Bureau, Ministry of Finance, 1967- . annual.

This report is the official yearly summary of Guyana's population and vital statistics.

199 **Report on the results of the census of the population, 1911.**
George D. Bayley. Georgetown: 'Argosy', 1912. 71p. Reprinted, Port of Spain, Trinidad: Central Statistical Office, 1966. (Reprints of Early West Indian Census Reports).

A report which was compiled by the Census Commissioner's Office, British Guiana. The reprint is a photographic reproduction of the original report, and was issued under the Census Research Programme of the Department of Sociology, University of the West Indies, and the Central Statistical Office of Trinidad and Tobago.

Population history

200 **Slave populations of the British Caribbean 1807-1834.**
B. W. Higman. Baltimore, Maryland; London: Johns Hopkins University Press, 1984. 781p. bibliog. maps.

A massive work of comparative analysis, which is based on quantitative data drawn from primary sources. Higman states that his aim is 'to provide a comprehensive analysis of the major demographic features of slavery in the British Caribbean between the abolition of the Atlantic slave trade in 1807 and the abolition of slavery in 1834.' Material on Britain's colonial possessions on the north coast of South America, Demerara-Essequibo and Berbice, 1807-1831, and on British Guiana after 1831, paints a grim picture of slavery on the Guianese plantations. The volume is divided into two parts: 400 pages of text narrate the population history of a slave society, and a 300-page statistical supplement presents the quantitative data.

201 **Movements in slave population of the Caribbean during the period of slave registration.**

G. W. Roberts. *Annals of the New York Academy of Sciences*, vol. 292 (June 27, 1977), p. 145-60. bibliog.

Utilizing the slave registration records introduced in the British colonies in the second decade of the nineteenth century, Roberts gathers together and analyses important data on the import and export of slaves in the British West Indian colonies. Much of his discussion centres on Guyana, 'since the Act of Slave Registration passed in Demerara and Essequibo in 1820 was one of the most comprehensive', providing data from which inferences on vital statistics for the slaves in the colony may be drawn.

202 **Factors involved in immigration and movements in the working force of British Guiana in the 19th century.**

G. W. Roberts, M. A. Johnson. *Social and Economic Studies*, vol. 23, no. 1 (March 1974), p. 69-83. bibliog.

A study of immigration and its effects in Guyana during the post-emancipation period, in which the authors consider 'the internal factors that stimulated immigration, the size of immigration and its impact on the country's labour force, some aspects of this labour force and the re-distribution of Guyanese population in the coastal region.'

203 **A new system of slavery: the export of Indian labour overseas 1830-1920.**

Hugh Tinker. London; New York: Oxford University Press, 1974. 432p. maps. bibliog.

The history of East Indian emigration to Guyana is included in this major work, described by its author as 'the first attempt to provide a comprehensive study of the whole process of emigration from rural India' during the nineteenth and early twentieth centuries.

204 **A history of Indians in British Guiana.**

Dwarka Nath. Foreword by Sir Gordon Lethem. London; New York: The Author, 1970. 2nd rev. ed. 281p.

In this revision of a book first published in 1950 Nath, himself an East Indian, emphasizes the achievements of this ethnic group without allowing his perspective to distort his presentation. His account of the history of the East Indians is informative, and enhanced by statistics. An indenture agreement is reproduced in an appendix.

205 **Summary statistics on indenture and associated migration affecting the West Indies, 1834-1918.**

G. W. Roberts, J. Byrne. *Population Studies*, vol. 20, no. 1 (July 1966), p. 125-34.

Tables pull together statistics on the migration, into Britain's Caribbean territories, of indentured labourers from India. The article also considers migrants from Madeira, Africa, China, Europe and other parts of the globe. Guyana received the first East Indian migrants (396 in 1838) and the largest number. In an appendix, the authors explain and evaluate the sources from which they have drawn their statistics.

206 **The establishment of the Portuguese community in British Guiana.**
K. O. Laurence. *Jamaican Historical Review*, vol. 5, no. 2 (Nov. 1965), p. 50-74.

This article analyses the causes of Portuguese upward-mobility in Guyana. Another study of Guyana's Portuguese community is Brian Moore's 'The social impact of Portuguese immigration into British Guiana after emancipation', *Boletin de Estudios Latinoamericanos y del Caraibe* (vol. 19 (Dec. 1975)).

207 **Some social characteristics of Indian immigrants to British Guiana.**
Raymond T. Smith. *Population Studies*, vol. 13, no. 1 (July 1959), p. 34-39.

'An analysis of the characteristics of a sample of East Indian indentured immigrants who entered British Guiana between 1865 and 1917 shows that the age, sex and caste characteristics of the immigrants are similar to those of East Indian migrants to other British colonies such as Fiji. The majority of the immigrants were Hindus belonging to the agricultural castes and on the basis of an analysis of recorded places of birth it is shown that approximately 85 per cent of all immigrants originated in the United Provinces and Bihar.'

208 **Some observations on the Chinese in British Guiana.**
Morton H. Fried. *Social and Economic Studies*, vol. 5, no. 1 (March 1956), p. 54-73. bibliog.

The report of a social scientist's survey of Chinese in British Guiana, which was conducted in the summer of 1954. Fried provides background information on the origins of the country's Chinese population, then delineates the main groups: the China-born ('home-born'), the Guiana-born (t'usheng), the Cantonese and the Hakka. Fried finds that Chinese ethnic identification has become attenuated among the Guyanese Chinese.

209 **Immigration of Africans into the British Caribbean.**
G. W. Roberts. *Population Studies*, vol. 7, no. 3 (March 1954), p. 235-62.

This thorough presentation of the facts on African immigration into the Caribbean area between 1841 and 1867 furnishes information on the flow of free Black settlers to British Guiana, where planters clamoured for plantation labour, and which received the major portion of such immigration. An appendix provides a discussion of the statistical sources upon which Roberts bases his figures and conclusions.

210 **A life table for a West Indian slave population.**
G. W. Roberts. *Population Studies*, vol. 5, no. 3 (March 1952), p. 238-43.

'This note comments briefly on the system of slave registration set up in the British colonies, and deals in particular with the data tabulated for the British Guiana slave population in the Parliamentary Papers, 1833. From the age distribution given there a life table has been constructed by a census differencing method. This life table shows the extremely high mortality then being experienced by slave populations in the West Indies.'

211 **Centenary history of the East Indians in British Guiana, 1838-1938.**
Peter Ruhomon. Georgetown: Daily Chronicle, 1947. 298p. (*Daily Chronicle*'s Guiana Edition of Reprints and Original Works Dealing With All Phases of Life in British Guiana, no. 10).

This volume, covering one hundred years of the history of the East Indians in Guyana, has a foreword by Sir Gordon Lethem.

212 **The introduction of East Indian coolies into the British West Indies.**
Edgar Erickson. *Journal of Modern History*, vol. 6, no. 2 (June 1934), p. 127-46.

This work offers a documented account of the vicissitudes of mid-nineteenth-century East Indian emigration to Britain's West Indian colonies. Erickson notes how this emigration, 'which began as a privately conducted enterprise in 1838, had, by about 1870, assumed definite form as a state-controlled enterprise'. He estimates that between 1851 and 1870 Guyana received 67,616 labourers from India.

213 **The Chinese in British Guiana.**
Sir Cecil Clementi. Georgetown: 'Argosy', 1915. 416p.

Clementi was Colonial Secretary of British Guiana, and administered the colony from 1916 to 1917, 1919 and 1921. His book is still a useful source for information on the colony's Chinese immigration and population, as Clementi had access to official documents. It is also imbued with Clementi's extensive knowledge of Chinese culture and language, gained in his previous assignment as deputy colonial secretary in Hong Kong.

Amerindians

214 **Individual and society in Guiana: a comparative study of Amerinidan social organization.**
Peter Riviere. Cambridge, Massachusetts: Cambridge University Press, 1984. 126p. map. bibliog. (Cambridge Studies in Social Anthropology, 51).

An ethnographic work that synthesizes published research on the social organization of Guyana's Amerindians. Riviere states that his book is designed both as an introduction to the ethnography of Guyana's indigenous tribes and as 'a contribution to the wider comparative study of the lowland South American society'. Guyana tribes included in the study are the Barama River Caribs, Akawaio, Macusi, Wapishiana and the Waiwai.

215 **Work opportunities and household organization among Barama River Caribs.**
Kathleen J. Adams. *Anthropos*, vol. 74, nos. 1 & 2, (1979), p. 219-22. bibliog.

A study considering the effect that employment in the gold mining industry has had on household organization and kinship relationships among the Barama River Caribs. According to the author, traditional relationships have been affected by economic factors stemming from industrial employment. Adams is also the author of a second study on the Barama River Caribs, 'The role of children in the changing socioeconomic strategies of the Guyanese Caribs' (*Canadian Journal of Anthropology/Revue Canadienne d'Anthropologie*, vol. 2, no. 1 [spring 1981], p. 61-66).

216 **American Indian or West Indian: the case of the coastal Amerindians of Guyana.**
Andrew Sanders. *Caribbean Studies*, vol. 16, no. 2 (July 1976), p. 117-44. bibliog.

'Amerindians in Guyana are the descendents of the aboriginal population and . . . are considered by other Guyanese to possess a non-Guyanese culture. This article attempts an examination of the relationship of Guyanese coastal Amerindian society and culture to that of tropical forest Amerindians of the Guianas on the one hand and of West Indian Creoles, and particularly Guyanese Creoles, on the other. A short account is first given of traditional Amerindian culture and institutions. This is followed by a more detailed account of contemporary Amerindian society and culture with a comparison with Guyanese Creole society culture.' The author analyses why certain traditional features have been maintained or lost, and why some aspects of Creole society have been incorporated into Amerindian culture.

217 **Amerindians in Guyana: a minority group in a multi-ethnic society.**
Andrew Sanders. *Caribbean Studies*, vol. 12, no. 2 (July 1972), p. 31-51.

This is an important summary of the political and social position held by Guyana's Amerindian minority in contemporary Guyanese society. Sanders discusses Amerindian attitudes towards the wider society and explains how Amerindian values both coincide with and differ from those held by Guyana's dominant groups. Sanders points out the stereotypes that Amerindians hold of other races, and also considers how other Guyanese view the Amerindians. The article includes a short history of the Amerindians and their relations with the ruling classes of Guyana over the centuries, and also mentions contemporary political initiatives undertaken by the Amerindians.

218 **The Guianas.**

Audrey J. Butt. *Bulletin of the International Committee on Urgent Anthropological and Ethnological Research*, no. 7 (1965), p. 69-90. maps. bibliog.

This article is an excellent review of anthropological research among the Amerindian tribes of all three Guianas. Butt locates the Amerindians, gives basic population and linguistic information and then summarizes recent ethnological research. Details of the publications on each tribe between 1935 and 1965 are provided and the possible orientation of future research is indicated. Both coastal and interior tribes of Guyana are covered. The bibliographies provided for each tribe show that in 1965 many tribes had not been studied since the 1940s.

219 **Material culture of the Waiwai.**

Jens Yde. Copenhagen: National Museum, 1965. 319p. (Nationalmuseets Skriften. Ethnografisk Raekke, no. 10).

An important ethnographic study of the agricultural economy of the Waiwai Amerindians, which is based on field-work conducted in 1958 and 1959.

220 **The gentle peopole; a journey among the Indian tribes of Guiana.**

Colin Henfrey. London: Hutchinson, 1964. 285p. maps. bibliog.

Skilfully-presented observations of the isolated Amerindian tribes, by a British undergraduate anthropological student. The book was published in the United States with the title *Through Indian eyes* (New York: Holt, Rinehart & Winston, 1965). Another book recounting travel among Guyana's Amerindians is W. M. Ridgwell's *Forgotten tribes of Guyana* (London: Tom Stacey, 1972).

221 **Ethnographic bibliography of South America.**

Timothy O'Leary. New Haven, Connecticutt: Human Relations Area Files, 1963. p. 329-31. maps. (Behavior Science Bibliographies).

Sections on 'Guiana', p. 329-30, and 'British Guiana', p. 330-31, provide listings of unannotated citations to books and periodical literature on the Amerindian tribes of Guyana. Other references are classified under the individual tribes. The bibliography is comprehensive, including work in all western languages. The Guyanese journal *Timehri* is indexed; thus, access is provided to the many articles on Guyana's Amerindians published in that important antiquarian journal.

222 **Waiwai: religion and society of an Amazonian tribe.**

Niels Fock. Copenhagen: National Museum, 1963. 316p. map. (Nationalmuseets Skrifter. Ethnogratisk Raekke, 8).

This scholarly study of Guyana's smallest Amerindian tribe was originally submitted as the author's doctoral thesis. Based on Fock's field work among the Waiwai in 1954-1955, it was the first full-scale anthropological study of the Amerindians in the Guianas to be completed since Gillin's 1936 study of the Barama River Caribs. The body of the work is in English, with a Danish summary. There are appendixes by Fridolen Weis Bentzon and Robert E. Hawkins.

223 **Symbolism and ritual among the Akawaio of British Guiana.**
Audrey J. Butt. *Nieuwe West-Indische Gids*, vol. 41, no. 2 (Dec. 1961), p. 141-61.

Using data gathered during two years of field-work, Butt analyses Akawaio modes of thought and the types of symbolism shown in their beliefs, rituals and everyday activities.

224 **The birth of a religion.**
Audrey J. Butt. *Journal of the Royal Anthropological Institute of Great Britain and Ireland*, vol. 90, no. 1 (Jan.–June 1960), p. 66-106.

This article offers an extended description of the Hallelujah religion of the Guyana Amerindians. Hallelujah was founded at the end of the nineteenth century by an Amerindian of the Macusi tribe, and was taken up by several other Guyanese tribes.

225 **Wai-wai; through the forests north of the Amazon.**
Nicholas Guppy. London: John Murray, 1958. 361p. map.

A first-person account of the tropical forest tribe, by a botanist who encountered these Amerindians while on a specimen-collecting expedition in Guyana and Brazil.

226 **Ritual blowing: 'taling' – a causation and cure of illness among the Akawaio.**
Audrey J. Butt. *Man*, vol. 56, nos. 48-60 (April 1956), p. 49-55.

Describes and analyses the practice of ritual blowing, which is used as both folk medicine and sorcery among the Akawaio of Guyana.

227 **Life among the Wai-Wai indians.**
Clifford Evans, Betty J. Meggers. *National Geographic Magazine*, vol. 107, no. 3 (March 1955), p. 329-46.

An excellent popular presentation of Amerindian life in the Guyanese interior, handsomely illustrated with twenty-two photographs, many in colour. The authors – a husband and wife team of archaeologists with wide experience in the region – visited a Waiwai village in order to explore archaeological sites, with the aim of determining the migration routes of prehistoric Amerindians and of charting the development of pottery-making and agriculture. At the same time, they observed present-day Waiwai and in this article they describe thêse Amerindians' daily life and arts and crafts.

228 **'The burning fountain whence it came'; (a study of the system of beliefs of the Carib-speaking Akawaio of British Guiana.)**
Audrey J. Butt. *Social and Economic Studies*, vol. 2, no. 1 (Sept. 1953), p. 102-16. bibliog.

Based on anthropological research done in 1951 and 1952, this is an intriguing and informative study of the system of religious beliefs held by Carib-speaking Akawaio in Guyana.

229 **Tribes of the Guianas and the left Amazon tributaries.**
John Gillin. In: *Handbook of the South American Indians, vol. 3: The tropical forest tribes.* Edited by Julian H. Steward. Washington, DC: GPO, 1948. maps. bibliog. (US Bureau of American Ethnology. Bulletin 143). Reprinted, New York: Cooper Square, 1963, p. 799-860.

This is an important synthesis of ethnographic information on the Guyanese Amerindians, as of the 1940s. Gillin provides a map locating both existent and extinct Indian tribes and lists tribal divisions, with references to anthropologic literature. He covers the history of the native peoples of the Guianas from 1590 to the 1940s and discusses the available ethnographic sources and the archaeology of the region. The major part of the text describes Amerindian culture, including: farming methods; hunting and gathering; fishing; food preparation; villages and houses; dress and ornaments; transportation; crafts and manufacturing; pottery; weapons; social and political organization; economic organization; life cycle; warfare; art, dance, music, games, and musical instruments; intoxicating beverages and narcotics; religion; magic and spirits; shamanism; lore and learning and etiquette. The comprehensive bibliography lists anthropological literature on the Amerindians, from the reports of early explorers through to the 1930s.

230 **The Barama River Caribs of British Guiana.**
John Gillin. Cambridge, Massachusetts: Museum, 1936. 274p. maps. bibliog. (Papers of the Peabody Museum of American Archaeology and Ethnology, Harvard University, vol. 14, no. 2). Reprinted, New York: Kraus Reprint, 1967.

The first major professional anthropological study of a Guianese Amerindian tribe, which is based on intensive fieldwork in Guyana. Gillin's book includes illustrations, diagrams and music.

231 **Crime and punishment among the Barama River Carib of British Guiana.**
John Gillin. *American Anthropologist*, vol. 36, no. 3 (July–Sept. 1934), p. 331-44.

An account of the law and justice system of the Carib groups living along the Barama River in the Northwest District of British Guiana, as Gillin observed them in the 1930s. The article includes some interesting information on Amerindian beliefs with regard to sorcery and the kanaima.

232 **Additional studies of the arts, crafts and customs of the Guiana Indians; with special reference to those of southern British Guiana.**
Walter E. Roth. Washington, DC: US Government Printing Office, 1929. 110p. bibliog. (Smithsonian Institution. Bureau of American Ethnology. Bulletin 91).

This publication is intended as an appendix to Roth's main work on Guyanese Amerindian arts, crafts, and customs (q.v.). Roth reports on an expedition he undertook to the southern area of Guyana from January to June, 1925, to study the Taruma and the Waiwai tribes. The sections in this sequel are keyed to those in the main work.

233 **An introductory study of the arts, crafts, and customs of the Guiana Indians.**
Walter E. Roth. In: *US Bureau of Ethnology, 38th Annual Report, 1916-1917.* Washington, DC: 1924, p. 23-745. maps. bibliog.

A massive and authoritative compilation of the arts, crafts and customs of Guyana's aboriginal inhabitants, as recorded by Roth from 1907 to 1921. The work is intended to complement Roth's earlier work on Amerindian animism and folklore (q.v.). The exhaustively detailed text is enhanced with over 341 illustrations.

234 **An inquiry into the animism and folk-lore of the Guiana Indians.**
Walter E. Roth. In: *US Bureau of American Ethnology, 30th Annual Report, 1908-1909.* Washington, DC, 1915, p. 103-386. bibliog.

This represents Roth's first study of the religion, mythology and folklore of the Guyana Amerindians.

235 **Among the Indians of Guiana; being sketches chiefly anthropologic from the interior of British Guiana.**
Everard F. Im Thurn. London: Kegan, Paul, Trench, 1883. 445p. map. Reprinted, New York: Dover, 1967.

Im Thurn recounts his nineteenth-century journey up the Essequibo into the Guyanese interior and presents detailed observations of the land and of its indigenous inhabitants as he found them at that time. Besides discussing the Amerindians' culture, religion and folklore, he includes interesting chapters on Indian antiquities and rock engravings.

236 **Legends and myths of the aboriginal Indians of British Guiana.**
Edited by the Rev. W. H. Brett. London: W. W. Gardner, 1880. 206p.

These Amerindian legends and folktales were collected and versified by the Rev. Brett. *Guiana legends*, a forty-nine-page pamphlet of tales collected by Brett and edited by Leonard Lambert was published in 1931 by the Society for the Propagation of the Gospel in Foreign Parts.

237 **The Indian tribes of Guiana; their condition and habits; with researches into their past history, superstitions, legends, antiquities, languages, etc.**
Rev. W. H. Brett. London: Bell & Daldy, 1868. 2nd ed. 500p. map.

The first edition of this work was published in New York in 1852. Brett was a missionary in the Pomeroon District in Guyana for forty years, and a pioneer in the study of the archaeology and the ethnography of Guyana's Amerindians. This is an autobiographical account of his encounters with the indigenous tribes during his missionary duties. It is a fascinating picture, not only of the mid-nineteenth century tribes but of the missionaries and their adventures in the tropical forest. It is also a compendium of detailed information about all aspects of the Amerindians' culture, which Brett recorded in minute detail, in spite of his expressed distaste for what he regarded as heathen superstitions.

238 **Sketches of Amerindian tribes, 1841-1843.**
Edward A. Goodall, with an introduction and notes by M. N. Menezes. London: British Museum Publications for the National Commission for Research Materials on Guyana, 1977. 88p.

A pictorial work that reproduces sketches of mid-nineteenth century Guyanese Amerindians drawn by the British artist Edward Goodall.

239 **Indian notices; or, sketches of the habits, characters, languages, superstitions, soil, and climate of the several nations; with remarks on their capacity for colonization, present government and suggestions for future improvement and civilization. Also the ichthyology of the fresh waters of the interior.**
William Hillhouse, with an introduction and notes by M. N. Menezes. Georgetown: National Commission for Research Materials on Guyana, 1978. new ed. 153p.

Reprints a work published in 1825. William Hillhouse was an English traveller and amateur ethnographer who severely criticized Great Britain's treatment of the Amerindians in her South American colony.

Emigration

General

240 **A bibliography of Caribbean migration and Caribbean immigrant communities.**

Compiled and edited by Rosemary Brana-Shute, with the assistance of Rosemarijn Hoefte. Gainesville, Florida: Reference and Bibliograpic Dept, University of Florida Libraries, in co-operation with the Center for Latin American Studies, University of Florida, 1983. 339p. (Bibliographic Series, no. 9).

This bibliography presents 2,585 unannotated citations on post-slave-trade population movements to and from the Caribbean area, including Guyana. Covers in-migration, intra-regional and out-migration, as well as related topics, such as acculturation. The main listing is alphabetical by author, with topical and geographic indexes. Approximately fifty references to Guyana are indexed. The citations were gathered through data base searches and refer to books, periodical articles and unpublished papers.

241 **Return migration to Guyana.**

A. J. Strachan. *Social and Economic Studies*, vol. 32, no. 3 (Sept. 1983), p. 121-42. bibliog.

Little is known about the number and type of migrants returning to the Caribbean. Strachan's study attempts to fill this knowledge gap through an analysis of return population movement to Guyana. Basing his work on a survey conducted by questionnaire, he assembles facts about the characteristics of Guyanese returnees. In the conclusion of his article he considers what the re-entering migrants mean in terms of Guyanese development, although he notes that returnees express a low level of satisfaction with conditions in their home country.

242 **The impact of brain drain on development: a case-study of Guyana.**
Martin J. Boodhoo, Ahamad Baksh. Georgetown: Ahamad Baksh Trust Fund; Manchester: International Trading Agency, 1981. 235p.

A study of the effect that the emigration of professional personnel has had upon Guyanese economic development. The authors note that educated Guyanese prefer to remain abroad largely because of the political situation in their home country. T. A. Pooran Singh and L. P. Rajraq gave research support to the authors.

Emigration to Great Britain and Guyanese in Great Britain

243 **Being a black bobby means hearing 'I'm sorry'.**
Joseph Lelyveld. *New York Times* (14 May 1986), p. 2.

This newspaper feature on Sgt. Andrew Simons, a London Metropolitan Police Officer and a native of Guyana, focuses on the tense racial atmosphere in which Sgt. Simons works.

244 **Select list of works on black immigration to Canada and Great Britain.**
In: *Black immigration and ethnicity in the United States; an annotated bibliography.* Center for Afroamerican and African Studies, University of Michigan. Westport, Connecticutt; London: Greenwood, 1985, p. 153-56. (Bibliographies and Indexes in Afro-American and African Studies, no. 2).

An unannotated list of books and periodical articles.

245 **New minorities, old conflicts: Asian and West Indian migrants in Britain.**
Sheila Allen. New York: Random House, 1971. 223p. maps. bibliog.

This study of race relations in England focuses on the problems faced by immigrants from Asia and the Caribbean area.

246 **West Indian migration to Great Britain; a social geography.**
Ceri Peach. London, New York: Oxford University Press, for the Institute of Race Relations, 1968. 122p. maps.

A short work dealing with Commonwealth immigrants in the United Kingdom.

247 **Black British: immigrants to England.**

R. B. Davison. London: Oxford University Press, for the Institute of Race Relations, 1966. 170p.

This study considers black emigrants from the Commonwealth, including the Caribbean, and the strains and stresses of their interactions with native Britons.

Emigration to the United States and Guyanese in the United States

248 **Black immigration and ethnicity in the United States; an annotated bibliography.**

Center for Afroamerican and African Studies, University of Michigan. Westport, Connecticutt; London: Greenwood, 1985. 170p. (Bibliographies and Indexes in Afro-American and African Studies, no. 2).

The main body of this work covers materials dealing with the immigration of peoples of African descent, from both the Caribbean area and directly from the African continent, to the United Sates. Included are bibliographies, literature surveys, general works on immigration and ethnicity and United States immigration legislation and policies, as well as items on particular black ethnic groups. References that include Guyanese can be located in the 'West Indians in the United States' section, p. 85-95. Roughly one-half of the entries in the volume are annotated.

Internal migration

249 **Urbanization in the Commonwealth Caribbean.**

Kempe Ronald Hope. Boulder, Colorado: Westview, 1986. 129p. bibliog.

Drawing his data from Barbados, Trinidad and Tobago, Jamaica and Guyana, Hope studies the causes and consequences of too-rapid urban population growth in the Commonwealth Caribbean, the result of unmanaged migration from rural areas. Hope ends his study with suggestions for ways of dealing with the problem.

250 **Labour migration and development in Guyana.**
Guy Standing, Fred Sukdeo. *International Labour Review*, vol. 116, no. 3 (Nov.–Dec. 1977), p. 303-13.

The authors are concerned with the migration of workers from Guyana's rural areas to the urban coastal strip, particularly Georgetown. Little is known about the causes of this rural exodus, although government studies of the phenomenon are underway. Standing and Sukdeo utilize data from population census returns and official statistics to provide basic information on the salient characteristics of internal migration in Guyana. They also examine the government programmes designed to reverse the rural-to-urban trend: the co-operative farming ventures, land settlement schemes and the Guyana National Service.

Folklore

General

251 **'Ef me naa bin come me naa been know'; social control and the Afro-Guyanese wake, 1900-1948.**
Brackette Williams. *Caribbean Quarterly*, vol. 30, nos. 3 & 4 (Sept.–Dec. 1984), p. 26-44.

In this article on Afro-Guyanese funeral customs, the author views the folk rituals performed at the wake as an organized means of social control. Such rituals played a key role as social sanctions in a Demerara village until 1948. The author provides descriptions of some of the folk games that were played as part of the wake, among them the Nancy Story and the Shell game, and also gives examples of several folk chants sung by mourners. The title of the article is Guyanese Creole English for 'Had I not come, I would not have known', and is the first line of the Nancy Story.

252 **Afro-American folk culture; an annotated bibliography of materials from North, Central, and South America, and the West Indies.**
John F. Szwed, Roger D. Abrahams, Robert Baron (et al). Philadelphia: Institute for the Study of Human Issues, 1978. 2 vols. (Publications of the American Folklore Society. Bibliographical and Special Series, vols. 31-32).

Folk culture is given the widest possible meaning in this bibliography, with the authors listing linguistic studies, songs, tales, games, historical studies and others. The main arrangement of the volume is geographical, indexed by both broad subject and locale. The English-speaking West Indies section in the second volume includes material on Guyana. Bibliographical details and short annotations describe books and periodical articles to 1973. Forty-nine journals in the folklore field were scanned for this bibliography.

253 **The fusion of African and Amerindian folk myths.**
Jan Carew. *Caribbean Quarterly*, vol. 23, no. 1 (March 1977), p. 7-21.

Carew, Guyanese novelist, poet and storyteller, first discusses the stories and storytellers that he heard during his childhood in his village of Agricola, then examines the 'important elements in the mytho-poetic traditions of the two parent cultures – the African and the Amerindian – from which the Guyanese folk myth derived'. In his article, he refers to the Mayan Popol Vuh, Amerindian beliefs and B'ra Anancy, the Spiderman, God, or Trickster of the African people, and shows how these mythic strands are woven together in Guyanese folklore.

254 **Dictionary of Guyanese folklore.**
A. J. Seymour. Georgetown: National History & Arts Council, 1975. 128p.

This dictionary offers definitions of Guyanese words pertaining to folklore.

255 **History, fable and myth in the Caribbean and Guianas.**
Wilson Harris. *Caribbean Quarterly*, vol. 16, no. 2 (June 1970), p. 1-32.

The text of the 1970 Edgar Mittelholzer Memorial lecture, also published separately by the National History and Arts Council, Georgetown. Harris discusses several topics, but his talk centres on the meaning of the limbo dance-anansi story in West Indian and Guyanese folklore.

256 **The shaping of folklore traditions in the British West Indies.**
Roger D. Abrahams. *Journal of Inter-American Studies*, vol. 9, no. 3 (July 1967), p. 456-80.

A lengthy and informative background discussion of the factors – historical, geographical, ecological, social and economic – that affected the formation and perpetuation of West Indian folklore as a whole, coupled with an analysis of the aesthetic patterns and forces that can be discerned in the region's folk culture. Guyana is included in the analysis, as Abrahams sees the country as part of the British Caribbean folk culture area.

257 **Chapters from a Guianese log-book; or, the folk-lore of sea coast and river life in British Guiana, comprising Indian, Boviander, and Negro life, habits, customs, and legendary tales with historic notes, political and natural.**
Charles Daniel Dance. Demerara: Royal Gazette, 1881. 360p.

The Rev. Dance describes folk beliefs and customs and retells folktales.

Proverbs

258 **The proverbs of British Guiana with an index of principal words, an index of subjects, and a glossary.**

James Speirs. Demerara: 'Argosy', 1902. 88p.

A collection of 1,070 proverbs in Guyanese Creole English, with a glossary defining over 300 words. A more recently published short work that includes Guyanese proverbs is Percy A. Brathwaite's and Serena U. Brathwaite's *Guyanese folklore: Guyanese proverbs and stories* (Georgetown: Brathwaite, 1967).

Folk medicine

259 **Integration of indigenous healing practices of the Kali cult with western psychiatric modalities in British Guiana.**

Philip Singer, Louis Aarons, Enrique Araneta. *Revista Interamericana de Psicologia*, vol. 1, no. 2 (June 1967), p. 103-13. bibliog.

An account of a co-operative project linking the Mental Hospital in Berbice and a nearby Kali cult temple. The project was begun in 1963 when five psychiatric patients from the hospital were taken to the temple for 'treatment' by traditional Kali healers. The article describes Kali diagnoses and therapy, and includes a brief case-study of a patient. The collaboration between doctors practising western psychiatric medicine and healers using traditional folk medical techniques has continued.

260 **The realm of the extra-human: agents and audiences.**

Edited by Agehananda Bharati. The Hague: Mouton; Chicago: Aldine, 1973. 556p. (International Congress of Anthropological & Ethnological Sciences, 9th, Chicago, 1973).

An essay on a Kali cult healer in Guyana, 'Learners of psychdynamics: history, diagnosis management, therapy by a Kali cult indigenous healer in Guyana', by Philip Singer, Enrique Araneta and J. Naido, is included in this collection.

Folk tales

261 **Afro-American folktales: stories from black traditions in the New World.**

Edited by Roger D. Abrahams. New York: Pantheon, 1985. 327p. bibliog.

This collection of folk tales was selected by Abrahams from published texts, and 'recast . . . in the standard vernacular of the American 'common reader', while attempting to maintain the cadences of the personal style of the storyteller and its local tradition of telling'. One tale from Guyana is included, 'Crawling into the Elephant's Belly', an Anansi tale found in Charles Daniel Dance's *Chapters from a Guianese Log-Book* (q.v.). Abraham's introduction to the tales is informative on the tradition of oral storytelling and oral performance in the Caribbean area.

262 **The third gift.**

Jan Carew. Boston: Little, Brown, 1974. 32p.

A Guyanese folk tale from an African source, recreated for children by a Guyanese novelist.

263 **Old time story; some old Guianese yarns re-spun by 'Pugagee Pungcuss'.**

G. H. H. McLellan. Edited by Vincent Roth. Georgetown: Daily Chronicle, 1943. 266p. (*Daily Chronicle*'s Guiana Edition of Reprints and Original Works Dealing With All Phases of Life in British Guiana, no. 7).

Comprises 314 anecdotes of Guyanese life that were originally published in the *Daily Chronicle* between 1937 and 1938.

264 **Essays and fables in the vernacular.**

Michael McTurk. Edited by Vincent Roth. Georgetown: Daily Chronicle, 1949. 97p. (*Daily Chronicle*'s Guiana Edition of Reprints and Original Works Dealing With All Phases of Life in British Guiana, no. 14).

Michael McTurk (1843-1915) was an Englishman who came to Guyana as a government surveyor and later became a magistrate. In the 1890s, under the pseudonym 'Quow', he published several collections of folk tales that he wrote in Guyanese Creole English. Roth's 1949 edition brings together tales from the earlier works.

Folk music

265 **Guiana sings.**

Vesta Lowe. Delaware, Ohio: Cooperative Recreation Service, 1959. 16p.

A collection of seventeen Afro-Guyanese songs, which is accompanied by an LP recording.

266 **Folk songs of Guyana; Queh-queh, chanties, & ragtime.**

Compiled by P. A. Brathwaite. Edited by Serena U. Brathwaite. Georgetown: C. A. Welshman. 1964. 24p.

This brings together the texts, without music, of twenty-one songs. The Brathwaites are also the authors of a booklet discussing traditional Afro-Guyanese music and musical instruments, entitled *Musical traditions: aspects of racial elements with influence on a Guianese community* (Georgetown: C. A. Welshman, 1962).

267 **Protest songs of East Indians in British Guiana.**

Ved Prakash Vatuk. *Journal of American Folklore*, vol. 77, no. 305 (July–Sept. 1964), p. 220-35.

'Protest songs' is the term Vatuk chooses to categorize a number of songs in creolized Hindi that he collected in British Guiana in 1962. These songs deal with the East Indians' trials and tribulations, both during the emigration and indenture period and later. 'All represent an expression of protest against the singers' lot in life, against changing times, and against a political and economic atmosphere in which freedom is lacking.' Vatuk provides examples of these songs and discusses their themes, pointing out how the songs reflect the East Indians' difficult life in Guyana.

Religion

Christianity

268 **Missionary methods and local responses: the Canadian Presbyterians and the East Indians in the Caribbean.**
Brinsley Samaroo. In: *East Indians in the Caribbean; colonialism and the struggle for identity: papers presented to a symposium on East Indians in the Caribbean, The University of the West Indies, June, 1975.* Preface by Bridget Brereton, Winston Dookeran, with an introduction by V. S. Naipaul. Millwood, New York; London; Nendeln, Liechtenstein: Kraus International, 1982, p. 93-115.

The Presbyterian Church of Nova Scotia started its missionary activity in the Caribbean in 1868, and extended it to Guyana in 1885. This article provides some very interesting anecdotes of the Canadian missionaries in the British Caribbean and of their evangelization efforts among East Indian Hindus and Muslims, including those in Guyana, during colonial days. In spite of their enthusiasm and dedication, as well as government encouragement, the missionaries failed to achieve the mass conversions at which they aimed.

269 **A short history of the Guyana Presbyterian Church.**
D. A. Bisnauth. Georgetown: Labour Advocate Printery, 1970. 91p.

This book traces the history of the Presbyterian Church in Guyana.

270 **Christ's witchdoctor: from savage sorcerer to jungle missionary.**
Homer E. Dowdy. New York: Harper, 1963; London: Hodder & Stoughton, 1967. 241p. maps.

The story of the work in the Guyana missions of Elka, a Waiwai Amerindian converted to Christianity, is told in this book.

271 **Paddles over the Kamarang; the story of the Davis Indians.**
Robert H. Pierson, Joseph O. Emmerson. Mountain View, California: Pacific Press, 1953. 110p.

An account of Seventh Day Adventist missions among the Akawaio, illustrated with photographs by the authors.

272 **Under the southern cross: a tale of love and missions.**
J. D. McKay. Pictou, Canada, 1914. 56p.

A posthumously published account of life and mission work among indentured East Indian labourers in Guyana, in the years 1903 to 1905. The Rev. McKay was a Canadian missionary who drowned in the Essequibo in 1905.

273 **The history of the London Missionary Society, 1795-1895.**
Richard Lovett. London: H. Frowde, 1899. 2 vols. maps.

It was the London Missionary Society that, at the request of a planter in Guyana, Hermanns H. Post, sent the first missionary, the Rev. John Wray, to the colony in 1808. The Society played an important role in the educational system of the country, which at one time was almost completely under its control. Volume two of Lovett's history covers the Society's activities in the West Indies and North and South America.

274 **The church in the West Indies.**
Alfred Caldecott. London: Society for Promoting Christian Knowledge; New York: E. & J. B. Young, 1898. 275p. map. bibliog. (Colonial Church History). Reprinted, London: F. Cass, 1970 (Cass Library of West Indian Studies, no. 14).

This work can still be used as an important source for the study of the history of Christianity in the Caribbean. Although Caldecott's book concentrates on the role of the Anglican Church in the region, he also gives a fair account of the work of non-conformist missionaries in the area.

275 **'The apostle of the Indians of Guiana'; a memoir of the life and labours of the Rev. W. H. Brett, BD, for forty years a missionary in British Guiana.**
Fortunato Pietro Luigi Josa. London: W. Gardner, Darton, 1888. 156p. map.

This biography of the Rev. William Henry Brett (1818-86) also provides important information on Protestant missions in South America.

276 **Mission work among the Indian tribes in the forests of Guiana.**
Rev. W. H. Brett. London: Society for Promoting Christian Knowledge; New York: E. & J. B. Young, 1881. 255p. map.

Brett went to Demerara in 1840 as a missionary from the Society for the Propagation of the Gospel. He became chaplain to the Bishop of Guiana and rector of Holy Trinity, Essequibo, between 1851 and 1879. This book presents a general description of the work of Brett and other missionaries among Guyana's Amerindian tribes.

277 **Ten years of mission life in British Guiana: being a memoir of the Rev. Thomas Youd.**
Rev. W. T. Veness. London: Society for Promoting Christian Knowledge, 1875. 136p. map.

The Rev. Youd was the first Protestant missionary to the Macusi Amerindians on the Essequibo River, first founding missions at Pirara and later at the Urwa rapids. His mission at Pirara was destroyed by the Brazilians, who saw him as the forerunner of British encroachment on territory claimed by Brazil. Youd's wife died at the Urwa rapids mission, perhaps poisoned by an Akawaio Indian.

278 **The missionary's wife: a memoir of Mrs. M. A. Henderson of Demerara by her husband.**
Thomas Henderson. London: John Snow, 1855. 114p.

The Rev. Thomas Henderson joined the Demerara branch of the London Missionary Society Guyana mission in 1838. This memoir of his wife, Mary Ann Leslie Henderson, was published shortly after her death in 1855.

279 **Missionary labours in British Guiana: with remarks on the manners, customs, and superstitious rites of the aborigines.**
Rev. J. H. Bernau. London: J. F. Shaw, 1847. 242p. map.

The Rev. John Henry Bernau, a missionary in the Bartica District, gives an account of the missions on the Essequibo.

Hinduism

280 **Religious belief and social change: aspects of the development of Hinduism in British Guiana.**
Chandra Jayawardena. *Comparative Studies in Society and History: an International Quarterly*, vol. 8, no. 2 (Jan. 1966), p. 211-240.

After a lengthy introduction explaining the social and religious situation among the East Indians in the Indian subcontinent prior to emigration to Guyana, the author traces the gradual but ultimately extensive changes that Hinduism and Indian cultural practices underwent in the colony. He notes that the caste system disintegrated and distinctive caste practices were abandoned. He also discusses the spread of Hindu reformists movements such as the Arya Samaj.

281 **Hindu marriage customs in British Guiana.**
R. T. Smith, C. Jayawardena. *Social and Economic Studies*, vol. 7, no. 2 (June 1958), p. 178-94. bibliog.

Based on field observations made in West Demerara and Berbice, this is 'an ethnographic account of the sequence of major events connected with an orthodox (i.e., Sanatan Dharm Maha Sabha) wedding in British Guiana', where, 'wedding ceremonies remain a focus of East Indian group consciousness'. The article covers the selection of a marital partner, betrothal (tilak), planting the nuptial pole, lawa ceremonies, the katha or sacred reading, the cooking of the marriage feast and the central marriage ceremony of the wedding.

Social Conditions

General

282 **The emergence of a multiracial society: the sociology of multiracism with reference to Guyana.**
Iris Devika Sukdeo. Smithtown, New York: Exposition Press, 1982. 224p. bibliog.

This is a study of the evolution of race relations in Guyana.

283 **Pluralism, race and class in Caribbean society.**
Stuart Hall. In: *Race and class in post-colonial society: a study of ethnic group relations in the English-speaking Caribbean, Bolivia, Chile and Mexico*. Paris: UNESCO, 1977, p. 150-82. bibliog.

This general discussion of the Anglophone Caribbean provides a good overview of the complex social structure, cultural pluralism and ethnic diversity to be found in the former British colonies. Hall argues that in the British-colonial-post-emancipation stage, these societies moved from a pre-emancipation caste system to a class structure, and in their present post-independence or 'decolonizing' stage, ethnic segments have become important. He states that, 'the work required to describe this 'decolonizing' national society . . . remains to be done'.

284 **West Indian societies.**
David Lowenthal. New York: Oxford University Press, 1972. 385p. map. bibliog. (American Geographical Society Research Series, no. 26).

A well-documented volume on the non-Hispanic societies of the West Indies that includes much information on Guyana. Lowenthal emphasizes the importance of race and colour in these societies, describing how they are organized in respect both to themselves and to the outside world. There are chapters on history, social structure, East Indians and Creoles, ethnic minorities, emigration and neo-colonialism and racial and national identity. The volume contains an excellent bibliography.

285 **Differential adaptations and micro-cultural evolution in Guyana.**
Leo A. Despres. In: *Afro-American anthropology; contemporary perspectives.* Edited by Norman E. Whitten, Jr., John F. Szwed. New York: Free Press, 1970, p. 263-87. map.

In this article, reprinted from *Southwestern Journal of Anthropology* (1969), Despres discusses the evolution of social and cultural adaptations in Guyana over a long period of time, from the nineteenth to the twentieth century. After an overview of the country and its geography, the author covers plantation, village and urban environments, and the adaptive strategies utilized by both Afro- and Indo-Guyanese in these three situations.

286 **Social stratification in the Caribbean.**
Raymond T. Smith. In: *Essays in comparative social stratification.* Edited by Leonard Plotnicov, Arthur Tuden. Pittsburgh: University of Pittsburgh Press, 1970, p. 43-76.

In his discussion of the unique features of Caribbean social structure, Smith compares Guyana with Jamaica with regard to the dominant role played by the 'race' issue in its politics.

287 **British Guiana: problems of cohesion in an immigrant society.**
Peter Newman. London; New York: Oxford University Press, 1964. 104p. map.

This expansion of the author's earlier article, 'Racial Tension in British Guiana' (*Race*, May 1962) provides a concise summary of the country's social structure, economy and politics in the 1950s and early 1960s, viewed in the context of its geography, natural resources and history.

Social structure

288 **A day in Babylon: street life in Guyana.**
David J. Dobb. *Caribbean Review*, vol. 10, no. 4 (fall 1981), p. 24-27 & 50.

An excerpt from a work in progress described by its author as an ethnographic and historical study of 'the culture and social structure of the black proto-proletariat in Georgetown, Guyana'. Based on fieldwork conducted from 1975 to 1978, this article provides a close description of life on a street in Albouystown, a run-down residential section of Georgetown.

289 **Class, status, and privilege: the objective interest of the new elite in Guyana.**
Ralph C. Gomes. In: *Caribbean issues of emergence: socio-economic and political perspectives*. Edited by Vincent R. McDonald. Washington, DC: University Press of America, 1980, p. 283-303. bibliog.

An essay that describes how the ruling class in Guyana handles competing demands and decides upon actions.

290 **Ethnicity and ethnic group relations in Guyana.**
Leo A. Despres. In: *The new ethnicity; perspectives from ethnology*. Edited by John W. Bennett. St. Paul: West, 1975, p. 127-47. bibliog. (Proceedings of the American Ethnological Society, 1973).

Despres discusses how ethnic groups relate to one another in Guyana on three social levels: the overall social system, ethnic group relations and individual ethnic encounters.

291 **Indian village in Guyana: a study of cultural change and ethnic identity.**
Mohammad A. Rauf. Leiden, Netherlands: Brill, 1974. 121p. bibliog. (Monographs and Theoretical Studies in Sociology and Anthropology in Honour of Nels Anderson. Publication 6).

Originally submitted as the author's thesis at Ohio Sate University in 1969, this is a study of the continuity of East Indian culture and ethnic identity across several generations of Indo-Guyanese living in the village of Crabwood Creek, Guyana.

292 **Relations between Indians and Africans in Guyana.**
Ved. P. Duggal. *Revista/Review Interamericana*, vol. 3, no. 1 (spring 1973), p. 55-60.

A short narrative summary of East Indian-African ethnic relations in Guyana. Although Duggal feels that group animosities have been exacerbated by vested interests, he believes that as Guyana develops industrially class distinctions will supersede ethnic differences.

293 **History, ecology, and demography in the British Caribbean: an analysis of East Indian ethnicity.**
Allen S. Ehrlich. *Southwestern Journal of Anthropology*, vol. 27, no. 2 (summer 1971), p. 166-80. maps. bibliog.

An inquiry into why East Indian culture patterns did not persist among East Indian immigrants to Jamaica, as they did in Trinidad and Guyana. Ehrlich compares the three countries, looking at the level of development of the plantation system, the natural environment and the adaptational patterns of the emancipated slaves. The ways that these three factors interacted in the three countries were quite distinct and thus affected the concentration or dispersal of East Indian indentured labourers. This, in turn, was crucial with regard to the retention or loss of East Indian culture.

294 **Incomplete transformation: social change in a Guyanese rural community.**

George E. Marcus. *Caribbean Studies*, vol. 9, no. 4 (Jan. 1970), p. 27-49.

A case study of the predominantly East Indian Guyanese village of Cane Grove, whose population underwent 'an economic transformation with a greatly lagging, corresponding social transformation', beginning in 1948 when a government land development project transformed the sugar estate labour force into small-holding rice farmers. Marcus's description of social conditions in the village is based on fieldwork undertaken in 1966 and 1967.

295 **Ideology and conflict in lower class communities.**

Chandra Jayawardena. *Comparative Studies in Society and History*, vol. 10, no. 4 (July 1968), p. 413-46. bibliog.

Jayawardena uses a community of East Indian plantation labourers in Guyana as an example in this essay dealing with 'the factors that contribute to the emergence of egalitarian ideologies, tracing the social processes they entail and analysing their consequences for social life'.

296 **Migration and social change: a survey of Indian communities overseas.**

Chandra Jawawardena. *Geographical Review*, vol. 58, no. 3 (July 1968), p. 426-49.

An essay that explores the changes induced among East Indians by emigration to the Caribbean countries, South Africa, East Africa, Mauritius, Ceylon, Malaya and Fiji. Jayawardena relates variations in the factors that came into play in the processes of emigration and initial settlement in these overseas regions to the extent of sociocultural changes that ocurred. Guyana is compared and contrasted with Fiji in relation to changes in the organization and practice of the Hindu religion among East Indian emigrants. The article is based on a review of published literature.

297 **Caste and identity in Guyana.**

Philip Singer. In: *Caste in overseas Indian communities*. Edited by Barton M. Schwartz. San Francisco: Chandler, 1967, p. 93-116. bibliog. (Chandler Publications in Anthropology & Sociology).

Singer studied Hindu rituals and ceremonies practised in Guyana in 1964 in order to make a 'case for the existence of a Hindu identity and personality in Guyana'. He concludes from his research that, among the country's East Indian Hindus, an awareness of caste plays a role in psychological identity, which is largely based upon familiarity with communal religious symbols and rites.

298 **Caste and social status among the Indians of Guyana.**
Raymond T. Smith, Chandra Jayawardena. In: *Caste in overseas Indian communities*. Edited by Barton M. Schwartz. San Francisco: Chandler, 1967, p. 43-92. bibliog. (Chandler Publications in Anthropology & Sociology).

Basing their opinions on their research in Guyana in the years 1956 to 1958, Smith and Jayawardena feel that the East Indian immigrants' absorption into a new social system in the colony led to the disintegration of the caste system among them. They point out that, in Guyana, caste restrictions regarding caste hierarchy, pollution, commensality and endogamy are ignored. At the same time, however, the cultural idiom of caste has persisted as a source of prestige applicable in a limited social context, although the main determinants of social status are the same for the Indo-Guyanese as for the wider society, being occupation, wealth and style of life.

299 **Conflict and solidarity in a Guianese plantation.**
Chandra Jayawardena. London: Athlone, 1963. 159p. (Monographs on Social Anthropology, no. 25).

An early major socio-anthropological study that gives a full and detailed account of social relations among Indo-Guyanese labourers.

Values and attitudes

300 **Political socialisation among adolescents in school – a comparative study of Barbados, Guyana and Trinidad.**
W. W. Anderson, R. W. Grant. *Social and Economic Studies*, vol. 26, no. 2 (June 1977), p. 217-33. bibliog.

An attempt 'to examine the 'state of affairs' in the crucial area of political learning . . . a preliminary analysis of several contingent areas without any attempt at grand theory.' Empirical data were drawn from the secondary school population in Barbados, Guyana and Trinidad. Students answered a questionnaire designed to show what they knew and how they felt about social changes.

301 **The identity question in plural societies: findings from Guyana.**
Omo Omoruyi. *Sociologus*, new series, vol. 26, no. 2 (1976), p. 150-61.

A paper about personal identity and national identity, based on data gathered from two types of Guyanese school settings, one an African-Indian mixed setting and the other exclusively African and exclusively East Indian. Omoruyi administered the Kuhn/McPartland test of self-identity to students in each of these settings. In this paper he analyses the results he obtained and draws conclusions from these results about the students' psychological commitments and patterns of socialization.

302 **Use of multiple symbols of association as a measure of cohesion in a plural society.**
Omo Omoruyi. *Sociologus*, new series, vol. 25, no. 1 (1975), p. 62-76.

A study of the sense of community versus dissociative attitudes in a developing and fragmented society. Omoruyi tested the responses to symbolic figures of a non-random sample of 250 students drawn from two types of Guyanese secondary schools in 1968 and 1969. From an analysis of the results of the test, Omoruyi comments that the students felt the competing pulls of religion and politics.

303 **Racial attitudes of Africans and Indians in Guyana.**
Joseph B. Landis. *Social and Economic Studies*, vol. 22, no. 4 (Dec. 1973), p. 426-39. bibliog.

Conducted in 1967, this survey of 456 East Indians and 372 Afro-Guyanese provides the quantitative, empirical data that were lacking in the literature on Guyanese racial attitudes. From the results of the survey, Landis concludes that 'Indians in Guyana tend to have superordinate racial attitudes towards Africans while Africans tend to have defensive attitudes towards Indians'.

304 **The prestige ranking of occupations: problems of method and interpretation suggested by a study in Guyana.**
Sara Graham, David Beckles. *Social and Economic Studies*, vol. 17, no. 4 (Dec. 1968), p. 367-80.

A discussion of the problems involved in interpretating data collected in a study of occupational ranking undertaken in Greater Georgetown in 1965 and 1966. Those taking part in the study were asked, 'to define groups consisting of occupations of similar prestige or standing'. A fold-out chart of occupations and their mean rank accompanies the text of the article.

305 **Hinduization and Creolization in Guyana: the plural society and basic personality.**
Philip Singer, Enrique Araneta, Jr. *Social and Economic Studies*, vol. 16, no. 3 (Sept. 1967), p. 221-36.

The authors, 'examine the phenomenon of overseas Indians in Guyana in terms of 'process' ', studying, 'the process of adaptive acculturation of a people as influenced by the prevailing social and economic institutions and resulting in a basic personality marked either by East Indian-Hindu characteristics or African-creole characteristics.' At the end of the article, the authors relate Creolization and Hinduization to 'Guyanization', stating that, 'If Guyanization is to rely less upon force, and more upon psychological and social sanctions, it will be necessary for the Africans and Indians to consider themselves more alike than different.'

Family, marriage, kinship and women

306 **Women as heads of households in the Caribbean: family structure and feminine status.**

Joycelin Massiah. New York: UNESCO, 1983. 69p. bibliog.

Guyana has the lowest proportion of female heads of household in the Caribbean, twenty-two and two-fifths per cent. In the Caribbean area, thirty-two per cent of all households are headed by women. Massiah presents comparative statistical data on this type of family organization as it is found in the region, profiling the female household head – her education, employment and occupation – and describing her survival strategies. The article also provides information on public benefits and financial assistance available to female-headed households.

307 **The status of women in Caribbean societies: an overview of their social, economic and sexual roles.**

Frances Henry, Pamela Wilson. *Social and Economic Studies*, vol. 24, no. 2 (June 1975), p. 165-99.

An extensive review of the published research literature on the women of the Caribbean region conducted, in the main by anthropologists in the areas of family studies'. Information on Guyanese women is drawn from the work of Raymond T. Smith.

308 **Family structure and domestic organization among coastal Amerindians in Guyana.**

Andrew Sanders. *Social and Economic Studies*, vol. 22, no. 4 (Dec. 1973), p. 440-78. bibliog.

'Coastal Amerindians are a creolised West Indian population which has not previously been studied and documented. The purpose of this paper is two-fold. Firstly, to remedy this deficiency by presenting data on Coastal Amerindians; and secondly and more specifically to examine Coastal Amerindian household and family structure and organization so that it may be added to the large body of data on Caribbean family structure and made available for comparative study. Thus the paper concentrates on kinship, the household, and grouping of households.' The study is based on fieldwork undertaken from 1965 to 1968.

309 **The East Indian family overseas.**

Leo David. *Social and Economic Studies*, vol. 13, no. 3 (Sept. 1964), p. 383-96. bibliog.

David draws on research material gathered in Guyana in his examination of what has happened to the Hindu family of Northern India since being transplanted to other societies. He looks at marriage phenomena, behaviour in the Indian household and certain other aspects of Hinduism such as ritual and caste. The traditional family pattern prevalent in India is described and the extent to which shifts in this pattern have occurred in overseas Indian communities is discussed.

310 **The family in the Caribbean.**
Raymond T. Smith. In: *Caribbean studies; a symposium*. Edited by Vera Rubin. Seattle: University of Washington Press, 1960, 2nd ed. p. 67-75. bibliog.

Smith discusses Caribbean family structure, using field data on household groups common in Guyana's black villages to illustrate his points. The article is followed by a commentary by John V. Murra.

311 **Marital stability in two Guianese sugar estate communities.**
C. Jayawardena. *Social and Economic Studies*, vol. 9, no. 1 (March 1960), p. 76-100. bibliog.

Jayawardena studied the two sugar estate communities of Blairmont and Port Mourant – whose population is largely East Indian – to determine the factors affecting marital stability. He concluded from his examination that 'conflicts that lead to marital instability in these two communities are closely related to the social system of each'. Jayawardena is also the author of 'Family organization on plantations in British Guiana' (*International Journal of Comparative Sociology*, vol. 3, no. 1 (1962)).

312 **Marriage and the family amongst East Indians in British Guiana.**
R. T. Smith, C. Jayawardena. *Social and Economic Studies*, vol. 8, no. 4 (Dec. 1959), p. 321-76. bibliog.

The authors studied three East Indian communities in Guyana in 1956, 1957, and 1958: the sugar estates of Blairmont and Port Mourant and the rice-cultivating settlement of Windsor Forest. Using the data from their field work, the authors provide a detailed analysis of the Guyanese East Indian family system, describing the East Indian household, marriage, and the kinship system.

313 **The negro family in British Guiana: family structure and social status in the villages.**
Raymond T. Smith. Foreword by Meyer Fortes. New York: Grove; London: Routledge & Kegan Paul, in association with the Institute of Social and Economic Research, University College of the West Indies, Jamaica, 1956. 282p. maps. bibliog. (International Library of Sociology and Social Reconstruction).

A socio-anthropological study, based on field-work carried out in three Guyanese villages, in 1951 to 1953. The first section of the volume is a thorough ethnographic description of Black rural households, kinship systems, and matrimonial patterns. In the second section, Smith generalizes from his data and attempts to view the Black rural family system in the context of Guyanese society.

Social Welfare and Social Problems

General

314 **Social security programs throughout the world, 1979.**
Office of Research and Statistics, Office of International Policy, Social Security Administration, US Department of Health and Human Services. Washington, DC: Government Printing Office, 1980. Rev. May 1980. 267p. (Research Report, no. 54; SSA Publication, no. 13-11805).

Prepared by the Comparative Studies Staff of the Office of International Policy, this publication has been issued periodically by the United States Social Security Administration since 1937. The volume reviewed here, issued May 1980, updates the edition of December 1973. Its purpose is, 'to assist those interested in comparing social security systems on an international basis.' Data are presented in tabular form, with brief discussions of the sources from which the information presented is drawn. The Guyana section, p. 98-99, covers the following types of social security programmes in that country: old age, invalidity, death; sickness and maternity; work injury; unemployment; family allowance. Information is provided as to the source of funds, qualifying conditions for benefits, cash benefits for temporary and permanent disability, survivor benefits, medical benefits for dependents, and the administrative organization of the programme.

315 **Poverty and basic needs: evidence from Guyana and the Philippines.**
Guy Standing, Richard Szal. Geneva: International Labour Office, 1979. 154p. bibliog. (A WEP Study).

This book consists of two long essays, one of which is Guy Standing's, 'Socialism and basic needs in Guyana', a study of Guyanese social policy in regard to the country's poor.

Crime, criminology and justice

316 **Domination and power in Guyana: a study of the police in a Third World context.**
George K. Danns. Foreword by Lewis Coser. New Brunswick, New Jersey: Transaction, 1982. 193p. bibliog.

A pioneering work, described by its author in his preface as, 'an effort to analyze and explain the emerging system of domination and the exercise of power in the Third World society of Guyana through a case study of the police, who illustrate the nature of rule in contemporary Guyanese society'. After a literature review and an overview of the organization of the Guyana Police Force, Danns considers the police in relation to politics, corruption, race, industrial unrest and the military. For a study of the pre-independence police force, see W. A. Orrett's *History of the British Guiana Police* (Georgetown: Daily Chronicle, 1951).

317 **Rule-making and rule-enforcement in plantation society: the ideological development of criminal justice in Guyana.**
David J. Dodd. *Social and Economic Studies*, vol. 31, no. 3 (Sept. 1982), p. 1-35. bibliog.

In this article, Dodd, 'outlines the growth and development of the criminal justice system in Guyana, showing how it traditionally supported the interests of the power elite in the colony and how it has continued to serve the interests of the ruling party (the PNC) in the post-Independence period.' He also, 'considers the issue of social control in the 'total institution' of the plantation and delineates the structure of its 'inmate' social system, which still provides both social types and role models and influences judicial proceedings, especially with regard to courtroom behaviour and popular sentiment. Finally, the argument is made that in spite of its formal pretensions, the criminal justice system has always been administered in an irrational and arbitrary manner, reflecting the workings of the political context in which it rests.'

318 **Crime, race and culture: a study in a developing country.**
Howard Jones. Chichester, England; New York: John Wiley, 1981. 184p. bibliog.

Jones uses quantitative data to compare the effects of various factors – economic, social, and demographic – on crime in Guyana.

319 **Crime in Guyana; some problems of comparative study in the Caribbean.**
Howard Jones. *Social and Economic Studies*, vol. 29, no. 1 (March 1980), p. 60-68.

Jones addresses the wide-spread perception of Guyana as a violent, crime-ridden, lawless society by comparing Guyanese crime statistics with similar data from England and Wales, Barbados, Jamaica, and Trinidad and Tobago. Statistics from 1965 to 1975 are utilized.

320 **Urban crime and violence in Guyana.**
Michael Parris. In: *Crime and punishment in the Caribbean.* Edited and introduced by Rosemary Brana-Shute, Gary Brana-Shute. Gainesville, Florida: Center for Latin American Studies, University of Florida, 1980. p. 105–13.

This article covers trends in crime in Guyana's three main urban areas: Georgetown, Linden and New Amsterdam. Parris, a Guyanese sociologist who has worked in the Guyanese Probation Service, comments on the role played by alcohol in criminal offences and on some rehabilitative measures that have been introduced to deal with offenders. Crime statistics for the three cities are presented in tabular form.

321 **A survey of the Guyanese prison population: a research note.**
Michael Parris. In: *Crime and punishment in the Caribbean.* Edited and introduced by Rosemary Brana-Shute, Gary Brana-Shute. Gainesville, Florida: Center for Latin American Studies, University of Florida, 1980. p. 105-13.

Parris details a proposal to conduct a survey of the Guyanese prison population in order to determine who goes to prison in Guyana. His article includes much factual information about the nation's prisons, the Guyana Prison Service and training programmes currently available to inmates.

Medicine and health care

322 **Giglioli in Guyana, 1922-1971.**
Denis Williams. Georgetown: National History and Arts Council, 1973. 68 & 16p. bibliog. (Library of Biography, 1).

A biography of Dr George Giglioli, Italian-born physician and expert in tropical medicine, who came to Guyana in 1922 and devoted his career to the eradication of malaria in the country.

323 **Thesis: cultural anthropology and community psychiatry; antithesis: World Health Organization and basic health services; synthesis: community development.**
Philip Singer, Enrique Oraneta. In: *Topias and Utopias in health: policy studies.* Edited by Stanley R. Ingman, Anthony E. Thomas. The Hague: Mouton; Chicago: Aldine, 1975, p. 335-56.

After a general discussion of the role of psychiatry *vis-à-vis* community development, the authors exemplify their main points in a section entitled 'Integrating a Psychiatric Service into a Community in Guyana', p. 348-56, which describes a project aimed at rehabilitating mental patients by integrating mental hospital activities into the social life of a nearby community.

324 **The development of medical services in British Guiana and Trinidad, 1841-1873.**
K. O. Laurence. *Jamaican Historical Review*, vol. 4 (1964), p. 59-67.

Laurence's study shows that the medical system in Guyana was established in order to provide care for indentured labourers, not the emancipated slaves.

Nutrition

325 **The national food and nutrition survey of Guyana.**
Pan American Health Organization. Washington, DC: Pan American Health Organization, 1976. 107p. (Scientific Publication, no. 323).

A survey of the diet and nutrition of the Guyanese people, jointly sponsored by the Guyanese government and the Pan American Health Organization, and conducted through the Caribbean Food and Nutrition Institute and the Food and Agriculture Organization of the United Nations.

Suicide

326 **Suicide and the communication of rage: a cross-cultural case study.**
Frederick D. McCandless. *American Journal of Psychiatry*, vol. 125, no. 2 (Aug. 1968), p. 197-205.

The report of a psychiatric study conducted in Guyana in 1965, at which time suicide attempts were considered a major public health problem with an estimated forty-three to seventy-five suicides per 100,000 population. Dr McCandless evaluated the case histories of thirty-six attempted suicides and concluded that, 'the incidence of suicide is lower among persons of African descent, which reflects the fact that there are a number of culturally sanctioned techniques for acting out hostile affects in this group. The East Indian, without a culturally accepted means for the discharge of aggression, can communicate his rage by directing it against himself.'

Politics and Government

327 **Guyana: politics, economy and society: beyond the Burnham era.**
Henry B. Jeffrey, Colin Baber. London: Pinter; Boulder, Colorado: Riemner, 1986. 203p. bibliog. (Marxist Régimes Series).

A study which is concerned with recent politics and class relations in Guyana.

328 **Guyana: politics and development in an emergent socialist state.**
Kempe Ronald Hope. Oakville, Ontario; New York; London: Mosaic, 1985. 136p. map. bibliog.

'This book is the culmination of research conducted in Guyana during . . . 1981-1985 . . . and is an attempt to describe, analyze, and interpret Guyana's political and economic history.' Hope concentrates on the effect of politics on the country's economic development, commenting that Guyana's experimental politico-economic system – co-operative socialism – has not been a success.

329 **Guyana: fraudulent revolution.**
Latin American Bureau. London: Latin American Bureau (Research and Action), 1984. 106p. bibliog.

An essay on the Guyana's recent political history that 'attempts to explain the process of disintegration and why the methods used by the imperial powers in the 1950s and 1960s to destroy the national movement for economic and political independence poisoned the life of the society for the next generation.' After a summary of Guyanese history, the book presents a grim account of Guyanese political life, which, it emphasizes, is, 'fundamentally a tale of fraud regularly punctuated by violence.' The volume also contains appendixes on the Guyana-Venezuela border dispute, on Jonestown and the House of Israel and on the role of the churches in Guyana.

330 **The rise of the authoritarian state in peripheral societies.**
Clive Y. Thomas. New York: Monthly Review, 1984. 157p. bibliog.

A leftist analysis of the nature of the state in recent post-colonial societies in the Caribbean and Africa, focusing on how and why so many newly independent states have developed into repressive dictatorships.

331 **The wild coast: an account of politics in Guyana.**
Reynold A. Burrowes. Cambridge, Massachusetts: Schenkman, 1984. 348p. bibliog.

A detailed history of Guyanese politics, 1950 to 1980. Burrowes covers the political manoeuvering prior to independence and the post-independence problems of development that continue to exacerbate the country's political situation.

332 **Bases of elite support for a regime; race, ideology, and clientelism as bases for leaders in Guyana and Trinidad.**
Percy C. Hintzen. *Comparative Political Studies*, vol. 16, no. 3 (Oct. 1983), p. 363-91.

Hintzen draws on, 'the attitudes, patterns of alignments, and composition of the most powerful and influential leaders in Guyana and Trinidad', in order to analyse, 'the racial, clientelistic, and ideological bases of regime support in the two countries.' In regard to Guyana, he finds that the ruling PNC party, 'is isolated from its 'natural' ideological constituency while at the same time, dependent upon the support [of] those elites who are ideologically opposed to the socialist direction of its policies.'

333 **Cooperativism, militarism, party politics, and democracy in Guyana.**
J. Edward Greene. In: *The newer Caribbean; decolonization, democracy and development.* Edited by Paget Henry, Carl Stone. Philadelphia: Institute for the Study of Human Issues, 1983, p. 257-80. (Inter-American Politics Series, vol. 4).

The author examines contemporary developments in Guyana, including co-operativism-militarism, the party system, the social bases underlying the organization of Guyanese society and the forms and effectiveness of democracy in the nation. Among the political parties and groups discussed are the People's National Congress (PNC), the Liberator Party, the People's Democratic Movement (PDM), the Association for Social and Cultural Relations with Independent Africa (ASCRIA) and other leftist groups.

334 **Race, ideology, and power in Guyana.**
Percy C. Hintzen, Ralph R. Premdas. *Journal of Commonwealth and Comparative Politics*, vol. 21, no. 2 (July 1983), p. 175-94.

The authors divide the recent political history of Guyana into four periods and relate the conditions underlying political power within these time-frames to Forbes Burnham's shifting espousal of ideologies.

335 **Decolonization and militarization in the Caribbean: the case of Guyana.**

George K. Danns. In: *The newer Caribbean; decolonization, democracy, and development.* Edited by Paget Henry, Carl Stone. Philadelphia: Institute for the Study of Human Issues, 1983, p. 63-93. bibliog. (Inter-American Politics Series, vol. 4).

'Perhaps the most conspicuous feature in Guyanese society over the last five years is the high visibility of uniformed military and paramilitary personnel.' This article discusses the growth in size and influence of this segment of Guyanese society and the rationale behind militaristic institutions. It covers the Guyanese Defence Force (GDF), the Guyana Police Force, the Guyana People's Militia, and the Guyana National Service.

336 **Guyana.**

William E. Ratliff. In: *Communism in Central America and the Caribbean.* Edited by Robert Wesson. Stanford, California: Hoover Institution, 1982, p. 141-50. (Hoover International Studies; Hoover Press Publications, 261).

Ratliff analyses Communism's appeal to the Guyanese, but finds race rather than ideology to be the crucial factor in the nation's politics. He provides an overview of the two major parties, Jagan's People's Progressive Party, a pro-Soviet Communist party, and Burnham's People's National Congress, and also covers the leftist-socialist Working People's Alliance. He discusses recent party policies, relations between Guyanese parties and international Communism, and contacts with the USSR.

337 **Guyana: coercion and control in political change.**

Percy C. Hintzen, Ralph R. Premdas. *Journal of Inter-American and World Affairs*, vol. 24, no. 3 (Aug. 1982), p. 337-54. bibliog.

A short article by two political scientists on authoritarianism in a post-colonial, communally-divided society, exemplified in Guyana by conflicts between Black and East Indian groups. The authors state that, 'while eroding human rights and short-circuiting democracy, [authoritarianism] ensures short-term political stability . . . but at the expense of economic development and natural autonomy.'

338 **People's power, no dictator.**

Walter Rodney, with an introduction by Trevor A. Campbell. *Latin American Perspectives*, issue 28, vol. 8, no. 1 (winter 1981), p. 64-78.

A reprint of Walter Rodney's last published work, a pamphlet published in 1979 that characterizes the Guyanese régime of Forbes Burnham as a dictatorship.

339 **Politics in ethnically bipolar states: Guyana, Malaysia, Fiji.**

R. S. Milne. Vancouver, Canada: University of British Columbia Press, 1981. 279p.

A comparative study of the political patterns of bipolar states, that is states where more than eighty per cent of the population are members of two major ethnic blocs. Typically, this situation results in the formation of ethnically-based parties. In Guyana, the blocs are composed of Africans and East Indians; in Malaysia, of Malays and Chinese and in Fiji, of Fijians and East Indians. Milne feels that the situation in Guyana is less intractable than in the other two countries.

340 **Jungle politics: Guyana, the People's Temple, and the affairs of state.**
Donald J. Waters. *Caribbean Review*, vol. 9, no. 2 (spring 1980), p. 8-13.

The author, an anthropologist and professor at Yale University, illuminates the connections between the Jonestown cult and Guyanese and international politics.

341 **Caribbean leftism.**
W. Raymond Duncan. *Problems of Communism*, vol. 27, no. 3 (May–June 1978), p. 35-57. map.

'Aside from Cuba's Communist Party (PCC), the only electorally significant Marxist-Leninist party in the Caribbean is Guyana's PPP, which has been recognized formally by the Communist Party of the Soviet Union (CPSU) and which attended the latter's 25th Congress in Moscow in March 1976 as a fraternal party.' Duncan analyses Guyana's two major political parties – both leftist – classifying the PPP as Marxist Leninist and the PNC as Caribbean socialist. He also discusses race as a political force in the country.

342 **Guyana: socialist reconstruction or political opportunism?**
Ralph R. Premdas. *Journal of Interamerican Studies and World Affairs*, vol. 20, no. 2 (May 1978), p. 133-64. bibliog.

'The purpose of this article is to identify the factors and analyze the processes that have led Guyana to adopt a socialist program to solve its problems of poverty and political power.' Premdas provides background information on the Burnham government, then examines the nationalization of major Guyanese corporations – two aluminium producers, Demerara Bauxite (DEMBA) and Reynolds Bauxite, and two sugar producers, Jessel Securities and Booker McConnell. His article ends with a discussion of the constraints militating against the internal implementation of a socialist programme.

343 **Politics, ethnicity and class in Guyana and Malaysia.**
R. S. Milne. *Social and Economic Studies*, vol. 26, no. 1 (March 1977), p. 18-37. bibliog.

This article seeks to compare the bases of parties and politics in two 'bipolar' states. Guyana and Malaysia are two countries where politics are organized along ethnic lines: Africans and East Indians in Guyana, Malays and Chinese in Malaysia.

344 **Guyana: communal conflict, socialism and political reconciliation.**
Ralph R. Premdas. *Inter-American Economic Affairs*, vol. 30, no. 4 (spring 1977) p. 63-83.

In this paper, ethnically-polarized Guyana serves as a model to exemplify the pattern of communal conflict in a multi-ethnic state. Premdas traces the country's political development since 1953, then considers its power structure in the 1970s. Drawing upon these data, he discusses, 'six patterns that may have general implications for communal politics in multi-ethnic societies.'

345 **The strange fate of a liberal democracy: political opposition and civil liberties in Guyana.**
E. E. Mahant. *Round Table*, no. 265 (Jan. 1977), p. 77-89.

Makes an assessment of political developments, race relations, nationalization and civil rights in Guyana. Noting that questionable electoral practices are common, and that the press has been curbed, Mahant views Guyana as poised between liberal democracy and authoritarianism.

346 **Civilian control of the military: implications in the plural societies of Guyana and Malaysia.**
Cynthia H. Enlow. In: *Civilian control of the military: theory and cases from developing countries.* Edited by Claude E. Welch, Jr. Albany, New York: State University of New York Press, 1976, p. 65-96.

Enlow, a political scientist, examines the politicization of the predominantly black Guyanese army and police, and what this implies in Guyana's bipolar ethnic situation.

347 **Guyana's socialism: an interview with Walter Rodney.**
Colin Prescod. *Race & Class*, vol. 18, no. 2 (autumn 1976), p. 109-28.

Rodney, the late political activist, intellectual, and government-opponent, explains his views on Guyanese politics and on the 'co-operative socialism' of the Burnham régime.

348 **The west on trial: the fight for Guyana's freedom.**
Cheddi Jagan. Berlin, German Democratic Republic: Seven Seas, 1975. Rev. ed. 435p. map.

Cheddi Jagan's autobiography, which was first published in 1966 with the title *The West on trial: my struggle for Guyana's freedom*. The reader is given some information about Jagan's personal life – growing up in British Guiana, dentistry study in the USA and marriage in 1943 to American Janet Rosenberg. However, the main emphasis is placed upon his political career. Required reading for students of the 1950s and 1960s when the Jagans and their People's Progressive Party were at the centre of Guyanese politics.

349 **The case of the missing majority.**
Ken I. Boodhoo. *Caribbean Review*, vol. 6, no. 2 (April–May–June 1974), p. 3-7.

Discusses the political situation in the early 1970s in Trinidad and Tobago and Guyana. 'Since no group in either the Trinidad or the Guyanese societies has a monopoly over power, these societies are comprised largely of 'minority groups'.'

350 **From colonialism to co-operative republic: aspects of political development in Guyana.**
Harold A. Lutchman. Rio Piedras, Puerto Rico: Institute of Caribbean Studies, University of Puerto Rico, 1974. 291p. (Caribbean Monograph Series, no. 9).

Considers the evolution of Guyana's constitutional and political system up to 1970, when, four years after achieving independence, the nation was organized as the world's first Co-operative Republic. The relationship between the country's two main contemporary parties, the government's PNC and the opposition PPP, is discussed.

351 **Competitive party organization and political integration in a racially fragmented state: the case of Guyana.**
Ralph R. Premdas. *Caribbean Studies*, vol. 12, no. 4 (Jan. 1973), p. 5-35.

'The aim of this article is to examine the role of competitive parties in the integration of an ethnically fragmented emerging nation. Its principal contention is that because many emerging nations are characterized by almost unsolvable internal divisions and disruptively rapid change, competitive parties formed around a nucleus of members from one or another sub-systems, such as a tribe or ethnic group, do not succeed in performing the function of integrating the state or in establishing legitimate political authority. Using Guyana as a test case, the article attempts to demonstrate the main hypothesis.'

352 **The recruitment of cabinet ministers in the former British Caribbean: a five-country study.**
Joel Gordon Verner. *Journal of Developing Areas*, vol. 7, no. 4 (July 1973), p. 635-52.

Guyana is one of the countries included in this study which surveys the selection of cabinet ministers from 1966 to 1971. Verner gathered his information from published sources and from correspondence with the people concerned.

353 **Guyana: socialism in a plural society.**
Paul G. Singh. London: Fabian Society, 1972. 24p. (Fabian Research Series, no. 307).

In this pamphlet, Singh analyses the socialist ideologies adopted by Guyanese political leaders: Fabianism, Jagan's Marxism-Leninism and Burnham's co-operative socialism.

354 **Elections and political campaigns in a racially bifurcated state: the case of Guyana.**

Ralph R. Premdas. *Journal of Inter-American Studies and World Affairs*, vol. 14, no. 3 (Aug. 1972), p. 271-96. bibliog.

Premdas contrasts Guyana's political system with integrated political systems. In the latter, elections serve to allow voters to reach a consensus. In Guyana, he finds, elections tend to intensify racial and ethnic divisions and, 'party competition evokes the most hostile intercommunity sentiment'. His article provides a description of the Guyanese party system and a record of voting participation since 1957, correlating race with voter preferences, and, 'a detailed analysis of campaign tactics, to show how they deepen racial cleavages between Indians and Africans in Guyana.'

355 **Race and political conflict in Guyana.**

Raymond T. Smith. *Race*, vol. 12, no. 4 (April 1971), p. 415-27.

'Guyana is the only western hemisphere country in which the descendants of immigrants from India constitute a majority of the population.' In this article, Smith argues, 'that while Guyana's racial structure has certainly provided the framework within which political conflict was expressed, that conflict does not arise in any simple way from the fact of racial and cultural diversity.' He examines the 1960s Jagan-Burnham political conflict and finds that foreign pressure and external control are the most important factors in Guyana's internal politics.

356 **A destiny to mould; selected discourses by the Prime Minister of Guyana.**

Forbes Burnham. Compiled by C. A. Nascimento, R. A. Burrowes. New York: Africana; London: Longman Caribbean, 1970. 275p.

Comprises a collection of Burnham's speeches, from 1955 through the 1960s. The discourses are arranged thematically according to the various political, national, and international issues on which he spoke. Each selection is prefaced by an explanatory passage describing the occasion for the speech. A thirty-five-page introduction written by the compilers – both of whom were Burnham's close associates – and six pages of plates showing Burnham with world leaders emphasize the partisan slant of the work.

357 **The cooperative republic of Guyana.**

Harold A. Lutchman. *Caribbean Studies*, vol. 10, no. 3 (Oct. 1970), p. 97-115.

A description of the changes introduced by the Guyanese government in 1970, as the nation changed from a monarchy to a republic. Covers modifications made in the executive and the judicial branches of the government.

358 **Guyana: race and politics among Africans and East Indians.**

Roy Arthur Glasgow. The Hague: M. Nijhoff, 1970. 153p. map. bibliog. (Studies in Social Life, no. 14).

Glasgow analyses the underlying ideologies that determine social and political behaviour in Guyana's two main electoral blocs.

359 **Legislative-executive relations in smaller territories.**
A. W. Singham. In: *Problems of smaller territories*. Edited by Burton Benedict. London: Athlone, 1967, p. 134-48. (Commonwealth Papers, no. 10).

Singham focuses primarily on the relationship between civil servants and elected ministers in British West Indian micro-states, but includes Guyana because, 'the basic problems are the same.' He discusses the fundamental disagreement between the two groups in the country over, 'the very nature of civil government,' which led to the suspension of the nation's constitution in 1953.

360 **The implications of nationalist politics in British Guiana for the development of cultural theory.**
Leo Despres. *American Anthropologist*, vol. 66, no. 5 (Oct. 1964), p. 1051-77. bibliog.

Despres delineates two theoretical models – the plural model and the reticulated model – that have been employed by anthropologists in the study of Caribbean societies, and utilizes each of these models in an analysis of data on nationalist politics in Guyana. He concludes from his analysis that neither model is adequate to explain the cultural change exemplified by the spread of nationalist politics – a change initiated by individuals for political ends and organized according to a calculated political strategy.

361 **The ordeal of British Guiana.**
Philip Reno. New York: Monthly Review, 1964. 132p. bibliog. map.

A pro-Jagan analysis of Guyanese politics in the crisis period of the early 1960s. Reno divides his volume into two sections, first discussing politics and recent history, then economic development. The work was first published as the July-August 1964 issue of the lefist periodical, *Monthly Review*.

Periodicals

362 **Guyana Information Bulletin.**
Edited by Janet Jagan. Georgetown, 1964- . monthly.

A monthly publication of the People's Progressive Party that follows human rights in Guyana.

363 **Guyana Journal.**
Edited by Lloyd Searwar. Georgetown, 1970- . quarterly.
A government publication, issued by the Ministry of External Affairs.

364 **Thunder.**
Edited by Clinton Collymore. Georgetown, 1969- . quarterly.
The quarterly journal of the People's Progressive Party.

Constitution, Law and Human Rights

Constitution

365 **West Indian constitutions: post-independence reform.**
Sir Fred Phillips. New York; London; Rome: Oceana, 1985. 370p. bibliog.

In a chapter entitled, 'Guyana Republican constitution socialist-style: Guyana revises drastically,' p. 53-72, Phillips prefaces his discussion of Guyana's 1980 Constitution with a review of the country's constitutional history, covering early constitutional arrangements, the constitutional developments of 1891, the Waddington Commission and the suspension of the constitution in the 1950s, and the Independence Constitution of 1966. After this prelude, he focuses on the 1980 Constitution, discussing its ideological basis, main provisions and specific articles. Other parts of the book are useful for broad comparison.

366 **Changing Caribbean constitutions.**
Francis Alexis. Bridgetown, Barbados: Antilles, 1983. 281p. bibliog.

This recent publication analysing constitutional evolution in Commonwealth Caribbean countries, 1962-1983, includes a substantial discussion of the changing nature of the constitution of Guyana, placed in a useful comparative context by the rest of the book.

367 **Constitution of the Cooperative Republic of Guyana Act 1980, Guyana Act No. 2 of 1980.**
Georgetown: Guyana National Lithographic, 1980. 135p.

Records the text of Guyana's present Constitution, promulgated October 6, 1980. This document greatly increased the power of the Executive Head of State.

368 **Constitutional development in Guyana, 1621-1978.**
M. Shahabuddeen. Foreword by L. F. S. Burnham.
Georgetown: Shahabuddeen, 1978. 685p. bibliog.

A history of the evolution of Guyana's constitutions, written by Guyana's Attorney General and Minister of Justice, Mohammed Shahabuddeen, with a foreword by Forbes Burnham, Guyana's first President.

369 **Freedom in the Caribbean: a study in constitutional change.**
Sir Fred Phillips. Foreword by E. V. Luckhoo. New York: Oceana, 1977. 737p. bibliog.

In Chapter XII of this volume, 'The rise of Republicanism: the Constitution of Guyana,' Phillips discusses the Guyana Independence Constitution of 1966, which was in force when this book was written. He points out the unique features of this Constitution, while noting that it has become unsatisfactory to Guyana's leader, Forbes Burnham. Other parts of the book have comparative relevance.

370 **Constitutional development of the West Indies 1922-1968; a selection from the major documents.**
Ann Spackman. St. Lawrence, Barbados; Epping, England: Caribbean Universities Press, in association with Bowker, 1975. 619p. bibliog.

Sections of interest for the study of Guyanese constitutional development are: 'A Description of the [1891] Constitution of British Guiana'; 'Documents dealing with the introduction of Crown Colony government in British Guiana, 1928'; 'The preamble to and extracts from the Guyana Constitution, 1966'; 'The suspension of the Constitution of British Guiana, 1953' and 'Bibliography of constitutional documents of the West Indies 1922-1968.'

371 **Constitutional change in the British West Indies, 1880-1903; with special reference to Jamaica, British Guiana, and Trinidad.**
H. A. Will. Oxford: Clarendon, 1970. 329p. bibliog.

The fifty-five-page section on British Guiana, from 1880 to 1895, traces the movement for constitutional reform that led to the Constitution of 1891 and discusses the provisions of this Constitution.

372 **The Constitution of Guyana and related constitutional instruments.**
Georgetown: Government Printery, 1966. 102p.

Presents Guyana's 1966 Independence Constitution.

373 **A constitutional history of British Guiana.**
Sir Cecil Clementi. London: Macmillan, 1937. 546p.

Sir Cecil Clementi was Colonial Secretary of British Guiana from 1913 to 1922. Although he was not a professional historian, his book is the standard work on Guyana's constitutional history up to 1928, covering the Dutch period, 1598 to 1803, and the subsequent period of British dominance. The text is supplemented by appendixes providing relevant documents from the eighteenth to the twentieth century.

Law and legislation

374 **A bibliographical guide to law in the Commonwealth Caribbean.**
Keith Patchett, Valerie Jenkins. Mona, Jamaica: Institute of Social and Economic Research, University of the West Indies, 1973. 80p. (Law and Society in the Caribbean, no. 2).

The publisher states that this book, 'Brings together comprehensive information on source material of interest to students and practitioners of law in the Commonwealth Caribbean. The entries are arranged under geographical and subject headings and an author and subject index is provided.'

375 **The legal system of Guyana.**
Mohammed Shahabuddeen. Georgetown: Guyana Printers, 1973. 523p. bibliog.

Guyanese law and legal procedures are modelled on the British common law system, with vestiges of Roman-Dutch law. This volume deals with the history of Guyana's law and its courts.

376 **The aborigines of British Guiana and their land.**
James Williams. *Anthropos*, vol. 31, (1936), p. 417-32.

Written at the time when Guyana was a British colony. Williams criticises the land-holding system under which the Amerindian tribes have no legal title to land that they have occupied for centuries. The article is a good summary of the attitudes of the region's colonizers – Spanish, Dutch, and British – towards the indigenous inhabitants' land rights.

Periodicals

377 **Guyana Law Journal.**
Georgetown: Department of Political Science and Law, University of Guyana, 1977- . semi-annual.

A publication covering various aspects of Guyanese law.

378 **The Official Gazette of Guyana.**
Georgetown. 1966- . weekly.

The official gazette of the Guyanese government, which began publication of Guyana's laws on May 28, 1966, shortly after independence. Prints legal notices and all legislation passed by the National Assembly. Some issues are accompanied by supplements.

Human rights

379 **Guyana.**

US State Department. In: *Country reports on human rights practices for 1986; report submitted on the Committee on Foreign Affairs, U.S. House of Representatives, and the Committee on Foreign Relations, U.S. Senate.* Washington, DC: US Government Printing Office, 1987, p. 524-32.

'In 1986 Guyana's human rights climate continued to show improvement.' This report, compiled by the US State Department from information furnished by US diplomatic missions abroad, Congressional studies, non-government organizations, and by the human rights bodies of international organizations, gives details of alleged recent human rights violations, while noting that the situation, particularly with regard to the opposition press, does not appear as grim as it once was. This report covers conditions up to the end of 1986.

380 **Human rights in Latin America, 1964-1980; a selective, annotated bibliography.**

Hispanic Division, Library of Congress. Washington, DC: Library of Congress, 1983. 257p.

The 'Caribbean (English-speaking)' section of this bibliography, p. 64-66, lists and annotates several items pertaining to the human rights situation in Guyana.

381 **The East Indians of Guyana and Trinidad.**

Malcolm Cross. London; New York: Minority Rights Group, 1980. 18p. bibliog. (Report of Minority Rights Group, no. 13).

A brief report on the effects of racial tensions on East Indians. This pamphlet is issued by an international human rights group that investigates discrimination and prejudice. It was first published in 1972 and reissued with revisions in 1980.

382 **The Akawaio, the upper Mazaruni hydroelectric project, and national development in Guyana.**

William Henningsgaard. Cambridge, Massachusetts: Cultural Survival . 1981. 37p. maps. bibliog. (Cultural Survival Occasional Paper, no. 4).

A pamphlet that adds new information to the 1978 Survival International report, *The damned* (q.v.), on the detrimental effects of the Mazaruni hydroelectric project on the Akawaio Amerindians.

383 **The damned: the plight of the Akawaio Indians of Guyana.**
Gordon Bennett, Audrey Colson, Stuart Wavell. London: Survival International, 1978. 12p. (Survival International Document, no. 6).

A strongly negative evaluation of the Guyanese government's planned hydro-electric project on the Mazaruni, which would displace the Akawaio Amerindians.

Administration and Local Government

384 **Local democracy in the Commonwealth Caribbean: a study of adaptation and growth.**
Paul G. Singh. Port of Spain, Trinidad; Kingston, Jamaica: Longman Caribbean, 1972. 146p. bibliog.

In this revised version of a doctoral thesis, Singh traces the changes that the transplanted British idea of local government underwent in Jamaica, Barbados, Guyana, and Trinidad up to 1968.

385 **Company towns in the Caribbean: a preliminary analysis of Christianburg-Wismar-Mackenzie.**
C. H. Grant. *Caribbean Studies*, vol. 11, no. 1 (April 1971), p. 46-72.

A lengthy study by a political scientist, 'of the social structure and the power configuration', of a company-created industrial town in Guyana, the bauxite-producing community of Christianburg-Wismar-Mackenzie. The author calls his article preliminary to a neglected aspect of research in mining operations in the Caribbean, but his presentation is extensive and detailed on the political institutions of the town.

386 **The ministerial system at work: a case study of Guyana.**
M. K. Bacchus. *Social and Economic Studies*, vol. 16, no. 1 (March 1967), p. 34-56.

This article on the Guyanese Civil Service first delineates the system of public administration as it was under British colonial government, then contrasts the past organization of the Civil Service with its post-independence structure and operation.

387 **Rural local government in Guyana and British Honduras.**
C. H. Grant. *Social and Economic Studies*, vol. 16, no. 1 (March 1967), p. 57-76.

A comparison of the systems of rural local government in the two Commonwealth Caribbean countries, as they were structured at the time that this article was written. Both systems, at that time, included the institution of the District Commissioner, a holdover from the British colonial administration.

388 **The civil service of British Guiana in the General Strike of 1963.**
B. A. N. Collins. *Caribbean Quarterly*, vol. 10, no. 2 (June 1964), p. 3-15.

Collins writes that, 'a most extraordinary feature of (the longest general strike in Commonwealth history, the 80-day strike that began April 20, 1963) was the part played by the British Guiana Civil Service.' A large portion of the membership of the Civil Service Association obeyed the strike called by the TUC in protest over the Jagan government's introduction of a Labour Relations Bill, although some members remained at their posts. Collins analyses the motives and attitudes of those who joined the strike and those who did not, and draws out the implications of these attitudes for the post-colonial Guyanese government.

389 **The approaches to local self-government in British Guiana.**
Allan Young. London: Longmans, Green, 1958. 246p. maps. bibliog.

Young's book is the most comprehensive study of the institutions of local government in Guyana under British colonial administration.

390 **Local government in British Guiana.**
Malcolm B. Laing. *Caribbean Quarterly*, vol. 1, no. 4 (1950?), p. 35-37.

A brief outline tracing the development of legislation authorizing institutions of local government in the colony.

Foreign Relations

General

391 **Border and territorial disputes; a Keesing's reference publication.**
Judith Bell, Henry W. Degenhardt (et al). Edited by Alan J. Day. London: Longman, 1987. 2nd ed. 462p. maps.

Updates information on Guyana's major foreign relations problems: its border disputes with its neighbours Suriname and Venezuela. Concise summaries of the history and current status of the controversies are given, for Guyana-Suriname, p. 431-34, and for Guyana-Venezuela, p. 435-38. A map showing the disputed areas can be found on page 329.

392 **Foreign policy behavior of Caribbean states: Guyana, Haiti, and Jamaica.**
Georges A. Fauriol. Lanham, Maryland: University Press of America, 1984. 338p. bibliog.

A scholarly study that makes an important contribution to the small amount of material available on the dynamics of foreign policy in the small, less-developed states of the Caribbean Basin. Fauriol applies a narrative treatment to the sources of Guyana's foreign policy and uses a quantitative analysis to explain output behaviour. This is a valuable book, both for its scholarship and for its interpretative power.

393 **Contemporary international relations of the Caribbean.**
Edited by Basil A. Ince. St. Augustine, Trinidad: Institute of International Relations, University of the West Indies, 1979. 359p. bibliog.

A recent collection of essays on Caribbean issues edited by an eminent Caribbean scholar and diplomat. Includes Dr Ince's own essay, 'Race and ideology in the foreign relations of independent Guyana: the case of the East Indians'.

394 **Perspectives from the Eastern tier: the foreign policies of Guyana, Trinidad and Tobago.**

Basil A. Ince. In: *The restless Caribbean; changing patterns of international relations*. Edited by Richard Millett, W. Marvin Will. New York: Praeger, 1979, p. 166-81. (Praeger Special Studies).

Ince contrasts the foreign policies of the two CARICOM Anglophone Caribbean states during the Williams-Burnham era. He divides Guyana's foreign relations into three periods. The first is 1966 to 1969, from independence to the demise of the coalition government. The second covers 1970 to 1976, from Lusaka to involvement in the Angolan Civil War. The third considers 1977 to 1979, Ambassador Andrew Young's visit and its aftermath. During each of these periods, Guyana's foreign policy shifted. Sections cover the two nations' relations with the following: the United States, the United Kingdom, and Western Europe; the Communist world; Latin America in general; Venezuela; Brazil; Mexico; and the Caribbean region. Ince places Guyana in the forefront of the nonaligned CARICOM nations.

395 **The Caribbean yearbook of international relations 1976.**

Edited by L. F. Manigat. Leyden: A. W. Sijthoff; St. Augustine, Trinidad: Institute of International Relations, University of the West Indies, 1977.

Includes two essays of interest to students of Guyanese foreign relations. These are, 'The Guyana/Surinam boundary dispute in international law,' by Duke E. Pollard, and 'Domestic political competition and foreign policy: Guyana's changing relations with the Communist world with special reference to Cuba, China and the Soviet Union,' by Henry S. Gill.

396 **Decolonization and conflict in the United Nations: Guyana's struggle for independence.**

Basil A. Ince. Cambridge, Massachusetts: Schenkmann, 1974. 202p. bibliog.

A study of the role played by the United Nations in the decolonization process as it took place in Guyana. Ince reviews politics in Guyana, 1953 to 1960, conflicts within the United Nations, British colonial practices and American policy in Guyana, 1953 to 1960, and United Nations practices and policies in relation to colonialism. The book ends with an assessment of the United Nations' contribution to Guyanese independence. Included in appendixes are United Nations documents which have bearing on the Guyanese independence issue.

397 **Foreign influence in Guyana: the struggle for independence.**

Colin V. F. Henfrey. In: *Patterns of foreign influence in the Caribbean*. Edited by Emanuel de Kadt. New York: Oxford University Press, 1972, p. 49-81. bibliog.

A detailed and well-researched account of British and American interference in Guyana's internal affairs during the past three decades. Of particular interest is Henfrey's documentation of the involvement of the Americans in defeating the Jagan régime in the early 1960s.

398 **Documents on international relations in the Caribbean.**

Edited by Roy Preiswerk. Foreword by Jacques Freymond. Rio Piedras, Puerto Rico: Institute of Caribbean Studies, University of Puerto Rico, 1970. 853p. bibliog.

A compendium that includes the texts of many documents pertaining to Guyana, among them the 'Award of the Tribunal of Arbitration on the Dispute between Great Britain and Venezuela, 3rd October 1899,' and the 'Statement on Guyana-Venezuela Relations by the Prime Minister of Guyana, the Hon. L. F. S. Burnham, to the National Assembly (and later circulated to U.N. Representatives) 12th July 1968.' Also includes documents on the Suriname-Guyana border dispute.

399 **Boundaries, possession, and conflicts in South America.**

Gordon Ireland. Cambridge, Massachusetts: Harvard University Press, 1938. 345p. maps. Reprinted, New York: Octagon, 1971.

An older work, but still a good source for those wishing to sort out the tangled history of the Venezuela–Great Britain–Guyana boundary claims, up to 1938. The section on Guyana, p. 230-243, traces the history of discovery and exploration in the region by the Spanish, Portuguese, Dutch, French, and British. According to Ireland, 'Great Britain by the treaty of August 13, 1814, obtained definite title to Berbice, Demerara, and Essequibo from the Netherlands'. Thus, when Venezuela gained her independence from Spain in 1830, the two countries carried an an old border dispute inherited from the Dutch and the Spanish. After a detailed presentation of the 1890s diplomatic negotiations pertaining to this conflict – in which the Americans as well as the British and the Venezuelans were involved – Ireland describes the 3 October 1899 Arbitration Commission award which determined the boundary line. On page 245, the details of the Great Britain–Netherlands conflict over the eastern boundary are given, a dispute which has now been taken up by Guyana and Suriname.

With African countries

400 **The Caribbean and Africa: a geo-political analysis.**

Linus A. Hoskins. In: *The Caribbean issues of emergence: socio-economic and political perspectives.* Edited by Vincent R. McDonald. Washington, DC: University Press of America, 1980, p. 147-69.

Hoskins examines the policies of Barbados, Guyana, Jamaica (under Manley), and Trinidad and Tobago in regard to Cuban involvement in Africa. Although these four countries have expressed their support for the liberation of Black Africans, and all except Barbados have endorsed armed struggle, only Jamaica has specifically supported Cuban intervention on the continent.

With countries of the Caribbean region

401 **Impulses and obstacles to Caribbean political integration.**
R. Stephen Milne. *International Studies Quarterly*, vol. 18, no. 3 (Sept. 1974), p. 291-316. bibliog.

Milne asks whether closer economic integration, as evinced by participation in a Caribbean Community and Common Market, will lead to political union in the Caribbean. Regarding this issue, he examines Guyana's role and its support for political integration in the Caribbean.

402 **Regional diplomacy of the Commonwealth Caribbean.**
Neville Linton. *International Journal*, vol. 26, no. 2 (spring 1971), p. 401-17.

A general discussion of foreign relations among the states of the Commonwealth Caribbean, in which Linton makes the point that although it has become characteristic of the region's diplomacy that emphasis is on direct dealings between prime ministers, this 'club' approach may prove inadequate in the future.

With Great Britain

403 **British Guiana: causes of the present discontents.**
Elisabeth Wallace. *International Journal*, vol. 19, no. 4 (autumn 1964), p. 512-44.

An objective presentation of the relations between Guyana and the United Kingdom in the pre-independence era of the 1950s and early 1960s. Wallace covers the negotiations between the UK and the Jagan government during the period.

404 **Europe in the Caribbean: the policies of Great Britain, France and the Netherlands toward their West Indian territories in the 20th century.**
Sir Harold Mitchell. Stanford, California: Hispanic American Society, Stanford University, 1963. 211p. maps. bibliog.

The author looks at the foreign policies of the colonial powers, and their political and economic aims at the end of the colonial period. Of interest in regard to Guyana are: Chapter three, 'The Caribbean Policy of Great Britain from 1815 to 1939'; Chapter seven, 'Problems of Closer Union in the British Caribbean' and Chapter nine, 'The Post-War British Economic Policy in the Caribbean'.

With the United States

405 **American labor and United States foreign policy.**
Ronald Radosh. New York: Random, 1969. 403p.

On pages 393-405, the author details the involvement of the American labour organization, the AFL-CIO, and the Central Intelligence Agency, in the eighty-day strike in Guyana that was instrumental in toppling the Jagan government – targeted as communist by Washington policymakers – in 1963. The remainder of the volume helps to place American involvement in the strike in context.

With Venezuela (boundary dispute)

406 **The Venezuela-Guyana border dispute: Britain's colonial legacy in Latin America.**
Jacqueline Anne Braveboy-Wagner. Boulder, Colorado: Westview, 1984. 349p. maps. bibliog.

This is the most recent modern study of the territorial issue of the Essequibo region, viewing the Guyana-Venezuela boundary conflict against the background of contemporary politics in the two countries. The following relevant documents are found in the appendixes to the text: Appendix A: Treaty of Arbitration, Great Britain and the United States, 1897, and Award of the Tribunal of Arbitration, 1899; Appendix B: Mallet-Prevost's Memorandum (extract) August 11, 1944; Appendix C: The Geneva Agreement (United Kingdom, British Guiana, and Venezuela), 1966.

407 **Which way out? A study of the Guyana-Venezuela boundary dispute.**
Leslie B. Rout, Jr. East Lansing, Michigan: Michigan State University, Latin American Studies Center, 1971. 1301. map. bibliog.

Discusses the claims of Venezuela and Guyana to the 53,000-square-mile area between the Orinoco and the Essequibo rivers. An interesting book, giving the history of the claims along with the personal views of the author.

408 **The Venezuela-Guyana boundary dispute in the United Nations.**
Basil A. Ince. *Caribbean Studies*, vol. 9, no. 4 (Jan. 1970), p. 5-26.

Against the background of the United Nations debates during the twenty-third session of the General Assembly (September-December, 1968), Ince discusses the long-lasting Venezuela-Guyana boundary dispute, considering its background; the genesis of the dispute in Venezuela's succession to Spanish claims in 1811 v. Great Britain's succession to Dutch territory by the Treaty of Paris in 1814;

Schomburgk's map of the British colony, drawn in 1839 and the Arbitral Award of 1899. He also considers the Mallet-Prevost Memorandum (1944), Venezuela's ostensible reason for reopening the case. He makes a perceptive examination of the arguments of both parties, the role of the United Nations, and the dynamics of the dispute in Guyana, Venezuela and the United Nations.

409 **The Venezuela-Guyana boundary arbitration of 1899: an appraisal. Part I.**

Cedric L. Joseph. *Caribbean Studies*, vol. 10, no. 2 (July 1970), p. 56-89. bibliog.

This article is the first of two in which Joseph evaluates the charges brought by Venezuela before the United Nations on 20 August 1962. In this action, Venezuela claimed that the 1899 Arbitral Award which settled her dispute with Great Britain over the Venezuela-Guyana boundary was concluded contrary to her interests because of a secret political 'deal' between Great Britain and Russia in which the principles of international law were disregarded. Joseph examines the oral and printed arguments for and against the claims of the two parties to the 1899 Arbitration, reviewing the history of the area from the Spanish discovery to the 1648 Treaty of Munster between Spain and the Netherlands. He also discusses the Mallet-Prevost memorandum of 8 February 1944, which, he contends, 'cannot contest the award of 1899'.

410 **The Venezuela-Guyana boundary arbitration of 1899: an appraisal. Part II.**

Cedric L. Joseph. *Caribbean Studies*, vol. 10, no. 4 (Jan. 1971), p. 35-74. bibliog.

Joseph continues his survey of the historical basis of the boundary conflict, discussing the possession of the disputed area up to the close of the Spanish period and during the periods of Dutch dominance and British control. He then discusses the 1899 Arbitration proceedings, concluding that, 'The award was a just one and in so complex a controversy compromise was essential'.

411 **Robert H. Schomburgk: explorador de Guayana y sus lineas de frontera.** (Robert H. Schomburgk: explorer of Guyana and his boundary lines.)

Pablo Ojer. Caracas, Venezuela: Universidad Central de Venezuela, Facultad de Haminades y Educacion, Instituto de Estudio Hispanoamericanos. 1969. 122p. maps. bibliog.

Ojer discusses Schomburgk's explorations in the Guyana interior between 1836 and 1843 and the map boundaries that he drew, in the context of the continuing border controversy between Venezuela and Guyana.

412 **The relevance of Latin America to the foreign policy of Commonwealth Caribbean states.**

Roy Preiswerk. *Journal of Inter-American Studies*, vol. 11, no. 2 (April 1969), p. 245-71.

Guyana's relations with Venezuela and the two nations' continuing boundary dispute are among the topics in this general discussion of the place of Latin America in Commonwealth Caribbean foreign policy. Preiswerk analyses the economic and political realities that account for Commonwealth Caribbean interest in Latin America as well as those that present obstacles to a *rapprochement* of the two regions.

413 **Report on the boundary question with British Guiana, submitted to the National government by Venezuelan experts.**
Herman Gonzalez-Oropeza, Pablo Objer. Caracas, Venezuela: Ministerio de Relaciones, 1967. 50p. maps.

This English translation of a work originally written in Spanish entitled *Informe que los expertos venezolanos para la cuestion de limites con Guayana Britanica presentan al Gobierno Nacional* explains the Venezuelan viewpoint on the boundary issue when it was revived at the United Nations during the 1960s.

414 **Tres momentos en el controversia de limites de Guayana; el incidente del Yuruan; Cleveland y la doctrina Monroe.** (Three moments in the controversy over the boundaries of Guyana; the Yuruan incident; Cleveland and the Monroe doctrine.)
Enrique Bernardo Nunez. Caracas, Venezuela: Imprenta Nacional, 1962. 2nd. ed. bibliog. (Publicaciones del Ministerio de Relaciones Exteriores).

A pro-Venezuelan view is expressed in this volume, comprising newspaper articles that were originally published in the Venezuelan journal *El Nacional* between 1944 and 1945. Nunez discusses and documents Guyana-Venezuela negotiations, from 1841 to 1890; the Yuruan incident of 1884 to 1885; the American role in the dispute and the resolution of the controversy by the 1899 Arbitration Award. There are two appendixes, on p. 107-15: 'El memorandum de Severo Mallet-Prevost' and 'El Presidente Betancourt y la revision de limites de Guayana'.

415 **The Venezuela-British Guiana boundary arbitration of 1899.**
Clifton J. Child. *American Journal of International Law*, vol. 44, no. 4 (Oct. 1950), p. 682-93.

A critique of the Mallet-Prevost memorandum published in *American Journal of International Law* in July, 1949. Basing his work on a close examination of the records of the arbitration proceedings and on contemporary newspaper reports, Child points out errors in Mallet-Prevost's account of the events of 1899. He also refutes the charge that a secret 'deal' was struck between Russia and Great Britain, noting that there is no evidence for it, and no basis existed at the time for such an event. In his opinion, the tribunal simply chose to follow diplomatic compromise rather than legal principles.

416 **The Venezuela-British Guiana boundary arbitration of 1899.**
William Cullen Dennis. *American Journal of International Law*, vol. 44, no. 4 (Oct. 1950), p. 720-27.

The author of this article backs up Mallet-Prevost's account of the events of 1899, as reported in his Memorandum of 1944, by stating that Mallet-Prevost had told him essentially the same story in 1910. Dennis summarizes the facts stated by Mallet-Prevost, which he believes have not been disproven. He agrees that the 1899 Arbitration judgment was unjudicial, being based on a diplomatic compromise.

417 **The Venezuela-British Guiana boundary dispute.**
Otto Schoenrich. *American Journal of International Law*, vol. 43, no. 3 (July 1949), p. 523-30.

Contained in this article is the 'Memorandum Left with Judge Schoenrich Not to Made Public Except at His Discretion After My Death', dictated by Severo Mallet-Prevost on 8 February 1944. Mallet-Prevost was a Spanish scholar and legal expert appointed to the 1899 Arbitration Trinunal which fixed the Venezuela-Guyana boundary. In his memorandum, Mallet-Prevost sets out his suspicions that the 1899 award was not made upon evidence presented before the tribunal, but was the result of a secret 'deal' negotiated between the Russian President of the Tribunal and its British members. When Mallet-Prevost died in December, 1948, Schoenrich, a junior partner in the New York firm of Curtis, Mallet-Prevost, Colt and Mosle, felt that the time had come to publish the memorandum. In his introductory paragraphs prefacing the memorandum, Schoenrich presents a strongly anti-British view of the dispute, giving details of the behind-the-scenes workings of the Arbitration Commission, and of the disappointment of the Venezuelans at the award.

418 **Latin America in maps: historic, geographic, economic.**
A. Curtis Wilgus. New York: Barnes & Noble, 1943. p. 296-97. maps. (College Outline Series).

On page 296 of this book appears a map showing the twelve demarcation lines that have been proposed at various times as the boundary between Guyana and Venezuela. A short text on the following page outlines the main points of the controversy.

419 **The Anglo-Venezuelan boundary controversy.**
Paul R. Fossum. *Hispanic American Historical Review*, vol. 8, no. 3 (April 1928), p. 299-329. map.

Focuses on United States involvement in the border dispute, noting that the Americans won an impressive diplomatic victory by successfully reasserting the Monroe Doctrine. Also accuses Venezuela of misrepresenting the facts of the case to the United States.

420 **Hispanic-American relations with the United States.**
William Spence Robertson. Edited by David Kinley. New York: Oxford University Press, 1923. 470p. bibliog. (Publications of the Carnegie Endowment for International Peace, Division of Economics and History, no. 21).

On pages 105-10 can be found a good summary of the American involvement in the Anglo-Venezuela boundary controversy and a discussion of President

Cleveland's invocation of the Monroe Doctrine as an issue in the dispute. Other parts of the book are of general interest.

421 **The search for the Venezuela-Guiana boundary.**
George Lincoln Burr. *American Historical Review*, vol. 4, no. 3 (April 1899), p. 470-77.

Burr, a member of the American Boundary Commission appointed by President Cleveland to investigate opposing claims to the Essequibo region, read this paper before the American Historical Association while the Arbitration Commission was debating the boundary issue. In it, he discusses his research in Dutch archives where he sought historical evidence for the boundary.

422 **Boundaries of British Guiana: the evidence of maps.**
Clements R. Markham. *Geographical Journal*, vol. 7, no. 3 (March 1896), p. 277-80 & 309.

A reprint – with some omissions – of Markham's communication to the London *Times* of 6 February 1896 regarding the cartographic evidence pertaining to the Great Britain-Venezuela-Guyana boundary dispute available in the map-room of the Royal Geographical Society. Markham, who was President of the Royal Geographical Society at the time, discusses early Spanish, Dutch and British maps of the region, and concludes from their evidence that Spain had no claim to Guyana and, therefore, Venezuela inherits no claim.

423 **The Venezuelan question: British aggression in Venezuela, or the Monroe doctrine on trial; Lord Salisbury's mistakes; fallacies of the British 'blue book' on the disputed boundary.**
William L. Scruggs. Atlanta, Georgia: Franklin, 1896. 91p. (US Commission Appointed to Investigate and Report upon the True Divisional Line Between Venezuela and British Guiana. Report, v. 9, no. 4).

Scruggs was American consul in Venezuela, before becoming legal adviser to the Venezuelan government. This work comprises three pamphlets that he wrote in support of the Venezuelan position regarding the disputed area. He argued that the British claim to the territory violated the Monroe Doctrine, a view that brought the United States government into the dispute.

Economics

General

424 **Foreign Economic Trends and their Implications for the United States: Guyana, November 1987.**
Prepared by the staff of the American Embassy, Georgetown. Washington, DC: US Dept. of Commerce, International Trade Administration, 1987. 13p. annual. (International Marketing Information Series).

Economic information is presented here with the American investor in mind. There is a table of economic indicators, a summary of economic conditions and a discussion of current economic trends. The volume covers the productive sectors of the Guyanese economy: sugar, bauxite, rice, gold and diamonds and other products; banking and investment; balance of payments and foreign debt and foreign aid.

425 **State capitalism in Guyana: an assessment of Burnham's Co-operative Socialist Republic.**
Clive Y. Thomas. In: *Crisis in the Caribbean*. Edited by Fitzroy Ambursley, Robin Cohen. New York: Monthly Review, 1983, p. 27-48. bibliog.

Guyana was declared a Co-operative Socialist Republic in 1970. Thomas outlines the features of this type of state, then discusses the production crisis that has been the primary feature of the Guyanese economy since the mid-1970s, and the repressive measures taken by the government to deal with the resulting social and political problems.

426 **Guyana: the IMF-World Bank Group and the general crisis.**
C. Y. Thomas. *Social and Economic Studies*, vol. 31, no. 4 (Dec. 1982), p. 16-70.

'In recent years the government of Guyana and the IMF-World Bank Group have been involved in many efforts to bring to a halt what has been termed, on several occasions, by both parties as the country's 'very serious financial and balance of payments crisis'. Because of their far-reaching significance for understanding both underdevelopment and Third World-IMF-World Bank Group involvements, this study explores a number of features of the relationship between the two parties and the crisis in Guyana. The first two sections introduce Guyana in a political economy context. This is followed by an analysis of the 'crisis' and the policy responses to it. The process of generalisation of the crisis is then analysed and (followed by) some concluding remarks.'

427 **Dependence, underdevelopment and socialist-oriented transformation in Guyana.**
James A. Sackey. *Inter-American Economic Affairs*, vol. 33, no. 1 (summer 1979), p. 29-50.

An analysis of the Guyanese economy which attempts to come to terms with its fundamental aspects, contending that, 'the development strategy of Guyana and its accompanying difficulties cannot be explained without reference to its state of dependence, class-formation and the conceptual ambivalence of the ruling Government'. In this article, Sackey covers radical decolonization and the persistence of external dependence, co-operative socialism and state capitalism, and the relations between state and class in the country, concluding that, 'in the immediate future, the direction of Guyana's development portends entrenchment within, rather than disengagement from, the web of international capitalism.'

428 **A macroeconomic assessment of the economy of Guyana.**
Kenneth P. Jameson, Frank J. Bonello. Washington, DC: Rural Development Division, Bureau for Latin America and the Caribbean, Agency for International Development, 1978. 84p. (Guyana, General Working Document, v. 3).

A report submitted to the United States Department of Agriculture and the Agency for International Development in April, 1978, which summarizes economic conditions in Guyana.

429 **Studies in post-colonial society – Guyana.**
Edited by Aubrey B. Armstrong. Associate editors: John Morris, Edward Turner, Roxanne Armstrong. Yaounde, Cameroon; Nashville, Tennessee: African World Press, 1975. 321p. bibliog.

A volume of essays that relate economics to social and political conditions in Guyana. Included are essays by Kempe Ronald Hope, 'Cooperativism, economic development and social change in a post-colonial society – Guyana'; Wilfred L. David, 'Comprehensive planning for national economic development: the Guyana experience' and Fred Sukdeo, 'Perspectives of cooperative socialism in the sugar industry.'

430 **The development of public enterprise in Guyana.**
Ethlyn A. Prince. Social and Economic Studies, vol. 23, no. 2 (June 1974), p. 204-15. bibliog.

A discussion of state intervention in the Guyanese post-colonial economy where government policy recognizes three economic sectors: private, public, and co-operative. 'State intervention . . . has taken the form of direct industrial participation, either by the acquisition of private industries by nationalisation or the creation of new state enterprises where previously there had been little activity . . .'. The author discusses the role of GUYSTAC, the Guyana State Corporation, in the economy.

431 **Ethnic difference and peasant economy in British Guiana.**
Raymond T. Smith. In: *Capital, saving and credit in peasant societies; studies from Asia, Oceania, the Caribbean and Middle America; essays.* Edited with two general essays by Raymond Firth, B. S. Yaney. Chicago: Aldine, 1964, p. 387-93. bibliog.

An examination of, 'the patterns of capital, savings and credit in the Guyanese coastal communities with special reference to the differences between Negro and Indian communities'. Based on Smith's fieldwork undertaken in three Black villages and one Indian village between 1951 and 1956.

432 **Inter-industry table for the economy of British Guiana, 1959, and national accounts, 1957-60.**
A. Kunda. Institute of Social and Economic Research, University of West Indies, Jamaica, 1963. 43p. (Supplement to Social and Economic Studies vol. 12, no. 1).

An inter-industry or input-output table of Guyana for 1959 (at the end of the Five-Year Development Programme). Kunda also brings up-to-date the set of national accounts for Guyana prepared by C. O'Loughlin for, 'The economy of British Guiana 1952-56,' (*Social and Economic Studies*, vol. 8, no. 1) (q.v.).

433 **The economy of British Guiana, 1952-56; a national accounts study.**
Carleen O'Loughlin. *Social and Economic Studies*, vol. 8, no. 1 (March 1959), p. i-226. map. bibliog.

This special number of the journal *Social and Economic Studies* presents the articulated accounts for Guyana for the years 1952 to 1956. At the same time, the work can be viewed as a study of the structure and growth of the country's economy during these years.

Economic history

434 **Power and economic change: the response to emancipation in Jamaica and British Guiana, 1840-1865.**
Philip J. McLewin. New York: Garland, 1987. 271p. bibliog.

A study of mid-nineteenth-century economic conditions, which centres on the supply of sugar workers.

435 **Plantations, peasants and state: a study of the mode of sugar production in Guyana.**
Clive Y. Thomas. Los Angeles, California: Center for Afro-American Studies, University of California; Mona, Jamaica: Institute of Social and Economic Research, University of the West Indies, 1984. 214p. (Afro-American Culture and Society, vol. 5).

A history of sugar production in Guyana in which Thomas analyses the plantation system under which sugar was produced and sold, and shows how the under-development of the Guyanese economy can be traced to this system.

436 **The plantation economy; population and economic change in Guyana, 1838-1960.**
Jay R. Mandle. Philadelphia: Temple University Press, 1973. 170p. bibliog.

An important economic history: Mandle sees the roots of Guyana's twentieth century underdevelopment in repressive colonial policies, designed to protect the sugar plantocracy from the necessity of paying competitive wages.

Sugar without slaves: the political economy of British Guiana, 1838-1904.
See item no. 152.

Planning and development

437 **Development policy in Guyana: planning, finance, and administration.**
Kempe R. Hope. Boulder, Colorado: Westview, 1979. 260p. bibliog.

The author, an economist formerly with the World Bank, analyses Guyana's economy from 1945 to 1976, and the Guyanese government's development policy, with the aim of determining whether this policy has contributed to the country's economic growth.

438 **Guyana: a bibliography on national development, 1966-1976.**
Mary Barta Thomas. Monticello, Illinois: Council for Planning Librarians, 1976. 49p. (Council of Planning Librarians. Exchange Bibliography, 1076).

A bibliography listing items dealing with economic conditions during the first ten years of Guyanese independence. Some of the entries are annotated.

439 **Guyana's second development plan 1972-76: a macro-economic assessment.**
Kempe R. Hope, Wilfred L. David, Aubrey B. Armstrong. *World Development*, vol. 4, no. 2 (Feb. 1976), p. 131-41.

A commentary on the Guyana's 1972-1976 Development Plan, written from a macro-economic point of view. The authors assess the Plan in terms of its applicability to the goals set for the Guyanese economy: the achievement of economic independence and self-sufficiency in food, clothing and housing.

440 **Planning for development in Guyana: the experience from 1945 to 1973.**
Kempe R. Hope, Wilfred L. David. *Inter-American Economic Affairs*, vol. 27, no. 4 (spring 1974), p. 27-46.

After an introduction explaining the structure of Guyana's economy and the philosophy behind the nation's planning, the authors, 'trace the evolution and ramifications of planning in Guyana from 1945-73 . . . assess its quality . . . analyze its merits and demerits', and make, 'some suggestions and recommendations for future planning'. The authors feel that early economic planners failed because they did not understand Guyanese society.

441 **The politics of economic planning in Guyana.**
J. E. Greene. *Social and Economic Studies*, vol. 23, no. 2 (June 1974), p. 186-203.

Makes an analysis of Guyana's variety of socialism, 'co-operative socialism'. Greene discusses the possibilities and problems inherent in this political philosophy when it is used as a basis for economic planning.

442 **Readings in the political economy of the Caribbean; a collection of reprints of articles on Caribbean political economy with suggested further reading.**
Edited by Norman Girvan, Owen Jefferson. Kingston, Jamaica: New World Group, 1971. 287p.

Includes Havelock Brewster's, 'Planning and economic development in Guyana', a commentary on the country's 1966-1972 Development Plan.

443 **The economic development of Guyana, 1953-1964.**
Wilfred L. David. London: Oxford University Press, 1969. 399p. map. bibliog.

A revision of the author's thesis, presented at Oxford University. David centres his economic study of Guyana on the problems of development. Among the topics covered are national income, population and employment, the agricultural and industrial sectors, finances, public expenditures and planning.

444 **The economic future of British Guiana.**
Peter Newman. *Social and Economic Studies*, vol. 9, no. 3 (Sept. 1960), p. 263-96.

A criticism of the government's proposed 1960-1964 Development Programme, which Newman felt would not solve British Guiana's economic and social problems.

445 **The economic development of British Guiana: report of a mission organized by the International Bank for Reconstruction and Development, at the request of the government of British Guiana.**
General Economic Survey Mission to British Guiana. Baltimore, Maryland: Johns Hopkins University Press, 1953. 366p.

A report of an examination of British Guiana's economy organized by the International Bank for Reconstruction and Development. The mission took place from 1 February to 16 March 1953. The report recommends development programmes for the country's agriculture, transport and communications, forestry, industry, education, health, housing, government and public administration.

Periodical

446 **Guynews.**
Georgetown: Ministry of Information and Culture, 1971- . monthly.

A government-issued magazine that reports economic news.

Investment, Finance and Banking

447 **An appraisal of the impact of recent changes in the rates of interest in Guyana.**
Raghubar Singh. *Social and Economic Studies*, vol. 31, no. 4 (Dec. 1982), p. 102-35.

A study of the recent economy of Guyana and its experiences with, 'a positive relationship between interest rates and savings, the balance of payments, investment and economic growth'. Singh first presents the theoretical arguments for higher interest rates in developing countries, then examines developments in the Guyanese financial system since 1978. He ends his article with, 'an attempt to rationalise these developments and to highlight other contributory factors'.

448 **Is size a disadvantage in dealing with transnational corporations?**
Frank Long. *Inter-American Economic Affairs*, vol. 33, no. 4 (spring 1980), p. 61-75.

A case study of foreign investment policies in Guyana from 1970 to 1979.

449 **Correlates of consumer banking behaviour in the Socialist Cooperative Republic of Guyana.**
Ivor S. Mitchell, Richard R. Still. *Social and Economic Studies*, vol. 29, nos. 2 & 3, (June & Sept. 1980), p. 56-88. bibliog.

The report of a study that was undertaken in Guyana in the 1970s with the aim of assisting the banking industry – particularly the Guyanese National Cooperative Bank – to understand the behaviour of the Guyanese banking customer. The article describes the banking system of Guyana and correlates bank customer behaviour with such socio-demographic factors as age, media use, education, income and ethnicity.

450 **The growth and structure of public expenditure and revenue in Guyana.**
John Gafar. *Caribbean Studies*, vol. 15, no. 3 (Oct. 1975), p. 138-148.

Gafar, an economist, analyses the growth and structure of Guyana's public expenditure and revenue between 1955 and 1971, in order, 'to identify the basic factors which have influenced aggregate public expenditure and revenue, that is [to determine] the relationship, if any, between national income and the level of public expenditure/revenue'.

451 **National cooperative commercial banking and development strategy in Guyana.**
Kempe R. Hope. *American Journal of Economics and Sociology*, vol. 34, no. 3 (July 1975), p. 309-22.

'The evolution of the cooperative movement in Guyana results in the adoption of a new development strategy. In it a leadership role is given to a new type of government bank, the Guyana National Cooperative Bank. Its mission is to protect and nurture the developing country's cooperative societies, organized mostly on Rochdale principles or on those of the Scandinavian marketing cooperatives. Basically a development savings bank, the GNCB is also an organ through which the Government is minimizing the role of foreign banks in the export sector of the national economy.'

452 **The political economy of indigenous commerical banking in Guyana.**
Compton Bourne. *Social and Economic Studies*, vol. 23, no. 1 (March 1974), p. 97-126. bibliog.

Bourne's paper attempts, 'to demonstrate that the appearance of indigenous commerical banks in the Caribbean is a conscious and deliberate political response to the economic failings of the expatriate banking system, as well as the expression of a desire for national independence.' Bourne analyses the performance and policies of the Guyana National Cooperative Bank, established in 1970.

Business and Non-Agricultural Industries

General

453 **Technology leasing as the latest imperialist phase: a case study of Guyana and Trinidad.**
Maurice A. Odle. *Social and Economic Studies*, vol. 1, no. 1 (March 1979), p. 189-233.

The author states that, 'technology leasing in the English-speaking Caribbean fits very much into the general framework of dependent underdevelopment.' His paper examines contractual arrangements in regard to technology leasing, with particular reference to manufacturing enterprises, the patent structure, the impact of the leasing process on government objectives and the alternatives to technology leasing facing developing nations. Data drawn from Guyana and Trinidad are used to exemplify the author's points.

454 **The aftermath of sovereignty: West Indian perspectives.**
Edited by David Lowenthal, Lambros Comitas. Garden City, New York: Doubleday/Anchor, 1973. p. 352-60. bibliog.

This volume includes Clive Y. Thomas's essay, 'Meaningful Participation: the Fraud of It', a discussion of how Guyana's steps towards nationalization of industry lack real efficacy.

Non-agricultural industries

455 **Guyana gold: the story of Wellesley A. Baird, Guyana's greatest miner.**

Wellesley A. Baird. Washington, DC: Three Continents, 1982. 185p. bibliog.

A biography of Wellesley Alfred Baird, a Guyanese gold miner. The book includes an essay by Kathleen J. Adams, an anthropologist, commenting on Baird's narrative.

456 **Conflicts between multinational corporations and less developed countries: the case of bauxite mining in the Caribbean, with special reference to Guyana.**

Thakoor Persaud. New York: Arno, 1980. 270p. bibliog.

This was originally submitted to Texas Tech University, in 1976, as the author's thesis. Persaud centres his paper on the conflict process as it occurs between multinational corporations and less developed countries, taking as an example one of the Caribbean's major extractive industries, the bauxite industry. He examines and analyses the historic record of conflict in this industry, then gives particular attention to the conflict between Guyana and Alcan Aluminium Ltd.

457 **Race, the political factor and the nationalization of Demerara Bauxite Company, Guyana.**

Maurice St.Pierre. *Social and Economic Studies*, vol. 24, no. 4 (Dec. 1975), p. 481-503. bibliog.

'This paper aims to present a sociological analysis of the dynamics of social change in MacKenzie which led to the nationalization of DEMBA. It is argued that the bauxite mining community as an active part of the colonial situation generated a number of strains for black Guyanese in particular, which led to various attempts at reduction. These were organized in such a way as to erode the very strong power base of DEMBA officialdom and thereby to create an atmosphere which facilitated the decision to nationalize.' St Pierre presents an interesting analysis of the 'company town' of MacKenzie and its structural racial separation. He also covers the process of unionization at DEMBA, and lists wildcat strikes that occurred in 1970.

458 **The role of private companies in the politics of empire: a case study of bauxite and diamond companies in Guyana in the early 1920s.**

Ann Spackman. *Social and Economic Studies*, vol. 24, no. 3 (Sept. 1975), p. 341-78. bibliog.

Spackman states that her article is, 'an attempt to marry the disciplines of political science and history, to describe and analyse the role of private companies in determining certain policy outcomes in the context of Imperial decision-making affecting the then colony of British Guiana in the 1920s.' Her essay centres on the activities of the Aluminium Company of America (ALCOA) and the Demerara

Bauxite Company (DEMBA) in the bauxite industry and the De Beers Company in diamond production and the attempts of these private companies to dominate their respective industries in Guyana. Spackman asserts that the companies were largely successful in imposing their interests on the government, even where the government sought to pursue a contrary policy. The article is based on research in Colonial Office papers.

459 **Political sequel to Alcan nationalization in Guyana: the international aspects.**
C. H. Grant. *Social and Economic Studies*, vol. 22, no. 2 (June 1973), p. 249-72. bibliog.

The government of Guyana nationalized the Demerara Bauxite Company (DEMBA) on 15 July 1971. Grant's article examines the political results of Guyana's attempt to gain control of its bauxite industry. In his analysis of the international repercussions of the nationalization, Grant focuses on the role of foreign banks and the World Bank.

Periodicals

460 **Guyana Business.**
Georgetown: Chamber of Commerce, 1968- . quarterly.

The successor to the *Commercial Review, Guyana Business* has a circulation of 1,000.

461 **Guymine News.**
Linden: Guyana Mining Enterprises, 1971- . monthly.

Formerly entitled *Guybau News*, this publication is the journal of the Guyanese mining industry. It has a circulation of 10,000.

Labour and Trade Unions

462 **Interest representation in the public service: a history of the Guyana Public Service Association.**
Harold A. Lutchman. Georgetown: Association, 1973. 309p. bibliog.

Traces the history of the Guyana Public Service Association, the trade union representing Guyanese government employees.

463 **Labour relations and industrial conflict in Commonwealth Caribbean countries.**
Zin Henry. Port of Spain, Trinidad: Columbus, 1972. 283p. bibliog.

Guyana is one of the countries included in this work on twentieth-century trade unions in the English-speaking Caribbean. Henry first traces the history of Caribbean trade unions, then discusses various factors in their development.

464 **Industrial unrest in MacKenzie, Guyana.**
Maurice St.Pierre. In: *McGill studies in Caribbean anthropology*. Edited by Frances Henry. Montreal: Centre for Developing Area Studies, McGill University, 1969, p. 65-80. (Occasional Paper Series, no. 5).

Traces the roots of industrial conflict in the bauxite industry to the belief that racial discrimination was practised by the Demerara Bauxite Company.

465 **Presidents and peons: recollections of a labor ambassador in Latin America.**

Serafino Romualdi. New York: Funk & Wagnalls, 1967. 524p.

On p. 345-52 of this book, Romualdi, the representative of the American trade union organization, the AFL-CIO, who visited Guyana, from 1953 to 1965, gives details of what he believes to have been world communist involvement in the Jagan government and of communist attempts to subvert Guyanese free trade unions during these years. The rest of the volume is useful for the reader interested in assessing Romualdi's views on Guyana.

466 **A history of trade unionism in Guyana, 1900-1961.**

Ashton Chase. Ruimveldt, Demerara: New Guyana, 1966. 327p.

A history of twentieth-century Guyanese working-class organization during the British colonial era. Information is provided on the British Guiana Labour Union (waterfront workers), the Manpower Citizens' Association (sugar workers), the Transport Workers' Union (railway and ferry workers), the Federation of Government Workers (public employees) and the British Guiana Bauxite Mine Workers' Union (bauxite miners).

Agriculture, Rural Conditions and Agricultural Industries

467 **Noncapitalist development: the struggle to nationalize the Guyanese sugar industry.**
Paulette Pierce. Totowa, New Jersey: Rowman & Allanheld, 1984. 200p. bibliog.

Based on the author's doctoral dissertation, this account of Guyanese development since independence focuses on, 'the transformation of the development strategy of the postcolonial state.' In particular, the book analyses, 'the process of radicalization which began in the late sixties and culminated in the nationalization of the property of Booker McConnell, Ltd., the oldest and largest expatriate company in the country.' Pierce deftly delineates the complex interplay of politics, development, and state ideology relevant to the nationalization of the sugar industry.

468 **Rich people and rice: factional politics in rural Guyana.**
Marilyn Silverman. Leiden, Netherlands: Brill, 1980. 240p. bibliog. (Monographs and Theoretical Studies in Sociology and Anthropology in Honour of Nels Anderson. Publication 16).

Based on research undertaken in an East Indian village in Guyana in 1969 to 1970, this study relates rural politics to economic development. For an earlier study of the economics of rice in an Indo-Guyanese community see R. T. Smith's 'Economic aspects of rice production in an East Indian community in British Guiana' (*Social and Economic Studies*, vol. 6, no. 4 (1957)).

469 **Plantation infrastructure and labor mobility in Guyana and Trinidad.**
Bonham C. Richardson. In: *Migration and development; implications for ethnic identity and political conflict.* Edited by Helen I. Safa, Brian M. DuToit. The Hague: Mouton, 1975, p. 205-26. bibliog. (World Anthropology).

Based on field research in Guyana in 1967 and 1968 to 1969, and in Trinidad in the summer of 1971. Richardson challenges the view that ethnic identity explains rural livelihood behaviour in these two countries. He believes that the plantation experience is the crucial factor behind both the historical and the contemporary economic behaviour of small-scale rural inhabitants in both territories.

470 **The rice economy of government schemes in Guyana.**
James W. Vining. *Inter-American Economic Affairs*, vol. 29, no. 1 (summer 1975), p. 3-20.

Guyana has a history of government-sponsored land settlement schemes dating from 1880. In this article, Vining looks at government-organized rice-producing projects, comparing the differences between such projects and individual rice output, in order to determine the factors that lead to success or failure in the rice schemes. The article includes a map showing active and defunct land settlement schemes.

471 **Rice, politics and development in Guyana.**
Eric R. Hawley. In: *Beyond the sociology of development: economy and society in Latin America and Africa.* Edited by Ivar Oxaal, Tony Barnett, David Booth. London; Boston, Massachusetts: Routledge & Kegan Paul, 1975, p. 131-53. bibliog.

Provides a, 'description and analysis of the Guyanese rice industry and the applicability of André Gunder Frank's model of metropolitan/satellite relationships.' (*Handbook of Latin American studies*).

472 **Distance regulation in Guyanese rice cultivation.**
Bonham C. Richardson. *Journal of Developing Areas*, vol. 8, no. 2 (Jan. 1974), p. 235-55. maps.

Richardson applies the von Thunen model to peasant-oriented rice-farm operations in Guyana. Richardson is also the author of 'Guyana's 'Green Revolution': social and ecological problems in an agricultural development programme' (*Caribbean Quarterly*, vol. 18, no. 1 (1972)).

473 **Population and economic change: the emergence of the rice industry in Guyana, 1895-1915.**
Jay R. Mandle. *Journal of Economic History*, vol. 30, no. 4 (Dec. 1970), p. 785-801.

In this case study of the economic influences generated by population growth in Guyana, Mandle applies a sophisticated analysis to the development of an agricultural industry. He demonstrates how the combination of a worsening sugar market and a government policy designed to stem the flow of labour back to India initiated the rice industry in Guyana in the late-nineteenth century.

474 **The decolonization of sugar in Guyana.**
Horace B. Davis. *Caribbean Studies*, vol. 7, no. 3 (Oct. 1967), p. 35-57.

A professor of economics at the University of Guyana discusses the Guyanese sugar industry at the beginning of independence. 'This paper attempts, first, to define what is meant by decolonization, and to dispose, by appropriate discussion, of some of the types that have been evoked; and, secondly, to examine, on the basis of experience that is only just becoming available, what exactly are the implications of a system of peasant cultivation of sugar lands.'

475 **Rice in the British Caribbean islands and British Guiana, 1950-1975.**
A. Kunda. *Social and Economic Studies*, vol. 13, no. 2 (June 1964), p. 243-81.

Gives a short description of Guyana's rice industry, covering supply and demand of rice, in the decade 1950 to 1960, and projects future trends in demand and supply of the commodity, from 1961 to 1975.

476 **Labour displacement in a labour-surplus economy: the sugar industry in British Guiana.**
Edwin P. Reubens, Beatrice G. Reubens. Mona, Jamaica: Institute of Social and Economic Research, University of the West Indies, 1962. 105p.

Based on field work done in 1961, this report analyses the labour force employed in the sugar industry, from 1949 to 1960, then projects future requirements in the light of technological improvements in sugar processing.

477 **The rice sector in the economy of British Guiana.**
C. O'Loughlin. *Social and Economic Studies*, vol. 7, no. 2 (June 1958), p. 115-43. bibliog.

The author's aim is to provide information on the economic structure of Guyana's rice industry. 'The first part of this paper incorporates a detailed analysis of the 'rice sector' in national income terms. The second part presents the tabulated results of a costing survey of 91 rice farms.'

Statistics

478 **Anuario Estadistico de America Latina y el Caraibe/Statistical Yearbook for Latin America and the Caribbean, 1985.**
Comision Economica para America Latina y el Caraibe/Economic Commission for Latin America and the Caribbean. New York: United Nations, 1986. 795p. annual.

An authoritative source for social and economic statistics on Latin America and the Caribbean region that includes figures for Guyana. The publisher states that, 'The First Part contains derived socio-economic indicators (growth rates, shares and coefficients or proportions). The Second Part contains the historical series in absolute numbers.' Tabular presentation of topical statistics facilitates comparison between countries.

479 **Statistical Digest.**
Georgetown: Statistical Bureau, Ministry of Economic Development, 1979- . annual.

A yearbook of economic statistics that continues and replaces the *Quarterly Statistical Digest*, formerly issued by the Statistical Bureau.

480 **Statistical Abstract of Guyana.**
Georgetown: Ministry of Finance, Statistical Bureau, 1970- . annual.

This is a yearly compilation of Guyanese statistics, focusing on economic and social statistics.

Education

481 **Education for development or underdevelopment? Guyana's educational system and its implications for the Third World.**
M. K. Bacchus. Waterloo, Ontario: Wilfrid Laurier University Press, 1980. 302p. bibliog. (Development Perspectives, Series 2).

Bacchus's volume links the organization and management of Guyana's schools to the nation's economic and social conditions.

482 **English in secondary education in a former British colony: a case study of Guyana.**
Dennis R. Craig. *Caribbean Studies*, vol. 10, no. 4 (Jan. 1971), p. 113-51.

A lengthy examination of Guyana's secondary school system in 1967, focusing on the problems of English language teaching. Craig discusses teaching methods, textbooks, and the language situation in Guyana *vis-à-vis* the non-standard English usages common in the country. The article concludes with recommendations for improvements in secondary pedagogy and with suggestions for university courses in English and for education courses in language teaching.

483 **A quantitative assessment of the levels of education required in Guyana by 1975.**
M. K. Bacchus. *Social and Economic Studies*, vol. 17, no. 2 (June 1968), p. 178-96.

Provides estimates of the types and levels of education – from primary school through to university – necessary to meet Guyana's needs in 1975.

484 **Problems to be faced in the use of English as the medium of education in four West Indian territories.**
Robert B. LePage. In: *Language problems in developing nations.* Edited by Joshua A. Fishman, Charles A. Ferguson, Jyotirindra Das Gupta. New York: Wiley, 1968, p. 431-42.

LePage directed the Linguistic Survey of the British West Indies, in the decade 1950 to 1960. In this brief paper, he characterizes the language problems besetting the educational systems of Jamaica, British Honduras, Guyana, and Trinidad and Tobago, and relates these problems to the social and psychological situation obtaining in these former British colonies. He then makes some suggestions for changes in teacher training to meet the needs and challenges of independence.

485 **Reports and repercussions in West Indian education, 1835-1933.**
Shirley C. Gordon. London: Ginn, 1968. 190p.

Gordon presents and discusses eight historical documents on West Indian education. She notes in her foreword to the volume that the reports that she has collected are all, 'official, [and in] all but one case . . . are the work of a commission to enquire into a special problem of the government of the time . . . they reveal the attitudes of the colonial administrations, supervised by the Colonial Office, in providing education for the West Indian colonies.' The volume is divided into three sections: 'The Reports and the Reporters'; 'The Main Topics of the Reports' and 'Extracts from the Reports'. The Report of the Commissioner of Education, British Guiana, 1925 (Major Bain Gray's Report) is included among the documents in the third section. This report was also published in the *Caribbean Quarterly* (vol. 10, no. 3 (Sept. 1964), p. 34-40) (q.v.).

486 **Documents which have guided education and policy in the West Indies: report of the Commissioner of Education, British Guiana, 1925.**
Shirley C. Gordon. *Caribbean Quarterly*, vol. 10, no. 3 (Sept. 1964), p. 34-40.

This is Major Bain Gray's annual departmental report, issued three months after he had taken up his appointment as Guyana's Commissioner of Education. Gordon characterizes this report as, 'one of the most forthright criticisms of a system of education in the British Caribbean ever to be issued.' Disliking many of the practices that he observed in the schools of Guyana, Major Gray set himself the task of raising the educational standards – particularly in regard to teacher qualifications – in the colony. Gordon provides a short introduction, extracts from the report, and a summary of its results.

487 **Secondary education in the Guianas.**
Louis W. Bone. Chicago: Comparative Education Center, University of Chicago, 1962. 70p. (Comparative Education Monographs, no. 2).

British Guiana is included in this, 'comparative study of the three Guianas with special reference to secondary education and economic development.' The volume provides data on the social structure of what were then British Guiana, Suriname, and French Guiana, while covering, 'the origins and growth of secondary education, recruitment and selection into the secondary schools, curriculum, teacher training and technical and vocational education.' Drawing on his study, Bone proposes steps which should be taken to spur the economic growth of the Guiana region.

488 **A history of the Queen's College of British Guiana.**
N. E. Cameron. Georgetown: F. A. Persick, 1951. 143p.

Queen's College, a secondary school founded in 1842, was the first school in Guyana. Among its alumni are such well-known Guyanese as A. J. Seymour, Walter MacArthur Lawrence, Wilson Harris, Martin Carter, Forbes Burnham, and Cheddi Jagan. The author of this history was the Deputy Principal of the school.

Language

489 **Dimensions of a Creole continuum: history, texts, linguistic analysis of Guyanese Creole.**
John R. Rickford. Stanford, California: Stanford University Press, 1987. 336p. bibliog.

A modern linguistic study of the varieties of Creole English spoken in Guyana.

490 **Dynamics of a Creole system.**
Derek Bickerton. London; New York: Cambridge University Press, 1975. 224p. bibliog.

The main thrust of Bickerton's work is to identify and describe successive mutations along the Guyanese-Creole-English continuum. A review of this book by Pauline Christie can be found in the *Caribbean Journal of Education* (vol. 3, no. 3 (Sept. 1976), p. 244-46).

491 **The nature of a Creole continuum.**
Derek Bickerton. *Language*, vol. 49, no. 3 (Sept. 1973), p. 640-69. bibliog.

A specialized article in which the copulative and the pronominal sub-systems of Guyanese-Creole-English are described in an attempt to construct a dynamic model of the continuum of a Creole language.

492 **Some sociolinguistic factors in the production of standard language in Guyana and implications for the language teacher.**
George N. Cave. *Language Learning*, vol. 20, no. 2 (Dec. 1970), p. 249-63. bibliog.

Cave gives a history and description of the speech forms prevalent in Guyana, tracing problems in the production of standard English in contemporary Guyana to the admixture of races and languages found in the Guyanese population. Cave reproduces examples of Guyanese-Creole-English speech – phonology, intonation, lexis, grammar – tape-recorded in 1969. He ends his article with a discussion of the pedagogic issue, stating his belief that, 'the language of the educated Guyanese [should be] the standard.'

493 **The English language in British Guiana.**
Richard Allsop. *English Language Teaching*, vol. 12, no. 2 (Jan.–March 1958), p. 59-66.

A brief article in which Allsop first outlines speech variation in the Guyanese population, then describes 'Creolese', giving its historical background and listing its main features. Allsop is also the author of 'Research in British Guiana Creole: methods and results,' published in *Language teaching, linguistics, and the teaching of English in a multilingual society*, edited by J. A. Jones (Mona: University of the West Indies, n.d.).

494 **Black talk, being notes on negro dialect in British Guiana, with (inevitably) a chapter on the vernacular of Barbados.**
J. Graham Cruickshank. Demerara: 'Argosy', 1916. 76p.

An early work considering the varieties of English spoken in Guyana. Cruickshank believes that the source of Guyanese Creole lies in the Creole English brought to the country in pre-emancipation days by slaves from Barbados, which combined with survivals from the Guyanese slaves' native African languages.

495 **The Creole tongue of British Guiana.**
J. Van Sertima. New Amsterdam, Berbice: Berbice Gazette Store, 1905. 60p.

This short discussion of Guyanese Creole English includes sample texts.

The Arts and Culture

496 **Cultural policy in Guyana.**
A. J. Seymour. Paris: UNESCO, 1977. 68p. (Studies and Documents on Cultural Policies).

One of a series of UNESCO-sponsored works aimed at providing comparative information on how cultural policies are planned and implemented in UN member states. Technical aspects of cultural policy are covered, including: evaluation of cultural needs, administrative and management structures, planning, financing, the roles of institutions, personnel training programmes, and other related subjects.

497 **Image and idea in the arts of Guyana.**
Denis Williams. Georgetown: Ministry of Information, National History and Arts Council, 1969. 39p. (Edgar Mittelholzer Memorial Lectures, 2nd series, 1969).

Denis Williams is Guyana's best-known painter. In this pamphlet he discusses his ideas about the arts in Guyana.

498 **Guiana.**
Philip J. C. Dark. In: *Encyclopedia of world art*. New York: McGraw Hill, 1963, vol. 7, p. 207-13. maps. bibliog.

In this summary article on the art of the three Guianas, Dark states that, 'The three principal manifestations of art [in the Guianas] are objects from archaeological sites, such as pottery, rock engravings, and rock paintings, certain decorative arts of the Amerinds – mainly featherwork, basketry, and beadwork, some pottery, and the art of the Bush Negro [of Suriname] principally wood carving.' The article includes sections on archaeological objects and Indian tribal art from Guyana and a map showing the location of petroglyphs and rock paintings in the country.

Co-operative republic: Guyana 1970; a study of aspects of our way of life.
See item no. 10.

I live in Georgetown.
See item no. 504.

Literature

General history and criticism

499 **Fifty Caribbean writers: a bio-bibliographical-critical sourcebook.**
Edited by Daryl Cumber Dance. Westport, Connecticut: Greenwood, 1986. 530p. bibliog.

A welcome compendium of information on twentieth-century Anglophone Caribbean writers. Each writer included receives an extended essay, prepared by a literary scholar, that covers his biography, major works and themes, critical reception, and honors and awards. This essay is followed by a bibliography listing both the subject's own works and critical studies. Guyanese writers included are: Jan Carew, Martin Carter, O. R. Dathorne, Wilson Harris, Roy A. K. Heath, Edgar Mittelholzer, A. J. Seymour, Eric Walrond and Denis Williams.

500 **Explorations: a selection of talks and articles, 1966-1981.**
Wilson Harris. Edited, with an introduction by Hena Maes-Jelinek. Mundelstrup, Denmark: Dangeroo, 1981. 145p. bibliog.

Guyana's leading novelist discusses Caribbean and Guyanese literature.

501 **West Indian literature: an index to criticism, 1930-1975.**
Jeannette B. Allis. Boston, Massachusetts: G. K. Hall, 1981. 353p. (Reference Publication in Latin American Studies).

Meticulous bibliographical work, covering writers, 'in the geographical region which includes those islands in the Caribbean Sea which were former British possessions (now independent nations) and Guyana'. There are three main sections: an index of authors, an index of critics and reviewers, and an index of general articles from 1933 onwards. Critical material in journals, newspapers and essay collections is located in this volume, which also includes single-author monographs and reviews.

502 **A companion to West Indian literature.**

Michael Hughes. London: Collins, 1979. 135p.

This work provides its readers with both biographical and bibliographical information on the writers of the English-speaking Caribbean.

503 **Bibliography of literature from Guyana.**

Robert E. McDowell. Arlington, Texas: Sable, 1975. 117p.

Besides listing poetry, drama, fiction and critical studies, this useful reference tool includes citations to memoirs, histories, newspapers, periodicals, anthropological works, folklore and travel books relating to Guyana. The bibliography is prefaced by A. J. Seymour's short essay, 'The Guyana National Bookshelf: a Mini-history of Literary Guyana', in which he calls the roll of those who have written about the country, from Sir Walter Raleigh's *Discovery of the large, rich and beautiful empire of Guiana* (q.v.) to the present day. Entries are arranged in an alphabetical author list, without annotations.

504 **I live in Georgetown.**

A. J. Seymour. Georgetown: Labour Advocate, 1974. 158p.

A collection of Seymour's essays and lectures on Caribbean and Guyanese civilization and literature: 'I live in Georgetown'; 'A personal approach to poetry'; 'The poetical imagination at work'; 'From Raleigh to Carew'; 'Cultural values in the Republic of Guyana'; 'Cultural background of the Caribbean'; 'Main currents in Caribbean literature'; 'The novel in the Caribbean'; 'The arts of the Caribbean'; 'Culture and Caribbean history' and 'Aspen and the American ethos'.

505 **The myth of El Dorado in the Caribbean novel.**

Hena Maes-Jelinek. *Journal of Commonwealth Literature*, vol. 6, no. 1 (June 1971), p. 113-28.

An interesting discussion of the theme that has haunted the West Indian – and particularly the Guyanese – imagination since Sir Walter Raleigh first sounded it in his *Discoverie* (q.v.): the myth of a golden city hidden in the South American jungle. Maes-Jelinek discusses this theme in several Caribbean writers, among them the Guyanese Edgar Mittelholzer, Jan Carew and Wilson Harris, in whose work El Dorado remains a key myth and 'as much a challenge as it ever was'.

506 **Critical writings on Commonwealth literatures; a selective bibliography to 1970, with a list of theses and dissertations.**

William H. New. University Park, Pennsylvania: Pennsylvania State University Press, 1975. 303p.

A bibliography that lists both general research aids for the study of Commonwealth literatures and criticism of individual authors. Guyanese writers included are: Martin Carter, Wilson Harris, Edgar Mittelholzer, Arthur J. Seymour and Denis Williams.

507 **The islands in between: essays on West Indian literature.**
Edited with an introduction by Louis James. London; Ibadan, Nairobi: Oxford University Press, 1968. 166p. bibliog.

James's forty-nine-page introduction links literature to the political and cultural situation in which the West Indian writer finds himself, a situation in which, according to James, the West Indian must 'search for his own voice'. Among the essays in the main body of the volume is John Hearne's 'The fugitive in the forest: a study of four novels by Wilson Harris', on pages 140 to 153.

508 **The unresolved constitution.**
Wilson Harris. *Caribbean Quarterly*, vol. 14, nos. 1 & 2 (March-June 1968), p. 43-47.

Harris discusses the West Indian novel, calling for it to move towards, 'an act of memory'.

Periodicals

509 **Kyk-Over-Al.**
Edited by A. J. Seymour. Georgetown: British Guiana Writers Association, 1945-61.

An important pioneering literary journal, founded by the editor, A. J. Seymour. It published fiction, poetry and critical essays. Many contemporary West Indian writers were first published in *Kyk-Over-Al.*

510 **Kaie.**
Georgetown: National History and Arts Council, 1965-73. annual.

This was the official journal of the National History and Arts Council of Guyana, a highly-regarded publication that featured articles of literary and intellectual interest.

Anthologies

511 **Breaklight; the poetry of the Caribbean.**
Edited with an introduction by Andrew Salkey. Garden City, New York: Doubleday, 1972. 265p.

An anthology of West Indian poetry that includes poems by Guyana's Jan Carew, Martin Carter, Ivan Van Sertima, A. J. Seymour, Wilson Harris, Slade Hopkinson, Wordsworth McAndrew and Milton Williams.

512 **My lovely native land.**
A. J. Seymour, Elma Seymour. Port-of-Spain, Trinidad: Longman Caribbean, 1971. 138p.

The diversity of Guyanese literature is illustrated in this collection which includes poetry, memoirs, essays and fiction, selected from the works of writers ranging from the Rev. John Smith to Lauchmonen.

513 **Island voices; stories from the West Indies.**
Selected with an introduction by Andrew Salkey. New York: Liveright, 1970. 256p.

Salkey, a Jamaican writer, provides a brief but insightful introduction to these twentieth-century short stories. Guyana is represented by authors Jan Carew, Edgar Mittelholzer, Denis Williams and O. R. Dathorne.

514 **Caribbean verse; an anthology.**
Edited with an introduction by O. R. Dathorne. London: Heinemann Educational, 1967. 131p. Reprinted, 1980.

Dathorne provides a fifteen-page introduction, charting the course of West Indian poetry from its beginnings to the present. Poems are annotated with critical notes (p. 82-121). Biographical notes (p. 122-28) identify the poets. There is an index of titles and first lines. Guyana's entries are: Martin Carter, 'University of Hunger'; Wilson Harris, 'Troy'; Walter MacA. Lawrence, 'Futility', 'Kaieteur'; Leo (Egbert Martin), 'The Swallow', 'Twilight' and A. J. Seymour, 'Sun is a Shapely Fire'.

515 **Caribbean narrative; an anthology of West Indian writing.**
Edited with an introduction by O. R. Dathorne. London: Heinemann Educational, 1966. 247p. Reprinted, 1979.

Representative selections from Anglophone West Indian imaginative prose writing, intended as an introduction to this work for 'younger readers at pre-University and University stage'. Dathorne's preface gives a brief sketch of West Indian prose from the *Letters* of Sancho (1782) to the 1960s. Excerpts from the following works of fiction by Guyanese writers are given: Jan Carew's *Black Midas* and *The wild coast* (q.v.); Wilson Harris's *Palace of the peacock* and *The secret ladder* (q.v.); Edgar Mittelholzer's *My bones and my flute* (q.v.) and *A tale of three places* and Denis Williams's *Other leopards* (q.v.).

516 **Guianese poetry (covering the hundred years' period 1831-1931).**
Selected and edited by N. E. Cameron. Georgetown: 'Argosy', 1931. 186p. Reprinted, Nendeln, Liechtenstein: Kraus Reprint, 1970.

A very important early collection of Guyanese poetry, prefaced by a twenty-page biographical and bibliographical essay by the editor.

Selected works of individual writers

E. R. Braithwaite

517 **To Sir, with love.**

E. R. Braithwaite. London: The Bodley Head, 1959. 187p.

Braithwaite's first book is an autobiographical account of his experiences as a secondary school teacher in the East End of London, from 1950 to 1957, where he taught disadvantaged students and faced racial discrimination. The book was made into a Columbia Pictures film starring Sidney Poitier.

Jan Carew

518 **Black Midas.**

Jan Carew. London: Secker & Warburg, 1958. 288p.

Carew's first novel features colourful Guyanese 'pork knockers', or prospectors. The American edition is entitled *A touch of Midas.*

519 **The wild coast.**

Jan Carew. London: Secker & Warburg, 1958. 256p.

Guyanese village life is the background for this novel. Carew is also the author of several books with non-Guyanese settings. *The last barbarian* (London: Secker & Warburg, 1961) depicts New York's Harlem and *Moscow is not my Mecca* (London: Secker & Warburg, 1964) tells the story of a black man in Soviet socialist society.

Martin Carter

520 **Poems of resistance from British Guiana.**

Martin Carter. London: Lawrence & Wishart, 1954. 18p.

In 1953 Carter was arrested and detained by the British for his radical political beliefs. It was during his term of imprisonment that he composed the poems in this pamphlet, expressing an intense and deeply felt protest against colonization and the colonizers. Among the best known poems are 'Till I Collect', 'Cartman of Dayclean', 'I come from the Nigger Yard', 'University of Hunger', and 'I Clench My Fist'.

Wilson Harris

521 **Tradition, the writer and society: critical essays, with an appendix by C. L. R. James.**
Wilson Harris. London: New Beacon, 1967. 75p.

A collection of Harris's essays in which he discusses literature and society. Harris has also published two further collections of critical essays: *Explorations* (q.v.), and *The womb of space: the cross-cultural imagination* (Westport, Connecticut: Greenwood, 1983).

522 **The Guyana quartet.**
Wilson Harris. London: Faber & Faber, 1985. 464p.

This is a one-volume edition of the four novels of Harris's tetralogy. The four novels are *Palace of the peacock* (1960), *The far journey of Oudin* (1961), *The whole armour* (1962) and *The secret ladder* (1963). Harris prefaces this edition with 'A Note on the Genesis of *The Guyana quartet*' in which he comments on his work.

Roy A. K. Heath

523 **A man come home.**
Roy A. K. Heath. Port-of-Spain, Trinidad: Longman Caribbean, 1974. 156p.

Heath's first published novel explored intense family relations in Georgetown. It attracted favourable critical attention.

524 **The murderer.**
Roy A. K. Heath. London: Allison & Busby, 1978; New York: Schocken, 1981. 190p.

Winner of the *Guardian* Fiction prize in 1978, this psychological novel charts the mental collapse of its protagonist.

Lauchmonen (Peter Kempadoo)

525 **Guiana boy.**
Lauchmonen (Peter Kempadoo). Crawley, England: New Literature, 1960. 172p.

The novel's protagonist, Lilboy, grows up on a Guyanese sugar estate, as did the book's author.

Walter MacArthur Lawrence

526 **The poet of Guiana, Walter MacA. Lawrence; selected works.**
Walter MacArthur Lawrence. Selected and edited by P. H. Daly. Georgetown: Daily Chronicle, 1948. 59p.

Thirty poems illustrating Lawrence's poetic production, with a biography of the poet by the editor.

Egbert Martin ('Leo')

527 **Poetical works.**
Egbert Martin. London: W. H. L. Collingridge, 1883. 224p.

Martin, who published under the pseudonym 'Leo', was Guyana's first important poet. Among his accomplishments was winning first prize in a competition to add two additional verses to the British National Anthem.

Edgar Mittelholzer

528 **Corentyne thunder.**
Edgar Mittelholzer, with an introduction by Louis James. London: Heinemann, 1970. 229p. (Caribbean Writers Series).

Mittelholzer's first novel, which is a lyrical presentation of the story of Ramgolall and his family. In his introduction to the book, Louis James notes that '*Corentyne thunder* was the first novel published that explored Guyanese peasant life', and describes it as, 'perceptive and delicate'.

529 **Children of Kaywana.**
Edgar Mittelholzer. London: P. Nevill, 1953. 515p. map. Reprinted, London: Secker & Warburg, 1960.

This is the first volume of Mittelholzer's major work, an epic trilogy that follows the fortunes of a Guyanese family, the Van Groenwegels, from the early seventeenth to the twentieth century. Sex and violence figure prominently in the saga, which begins in the first book with the meeting between Kaywana, a woman of Amerindian and English blood, and her Dutch lover.

530 **The harrowing of Hubertus.**
Edgar Mittelholzer. London: Secker & Warburg, 1954. 303p.

The second novel in the *Kaywana Trilogy* centres on Hubertus van Groenwegel and his struggles to overcome the violence inherent in his ancestry. The narrative follows his life from his birth in 1727 to his death in the early 1800s.

531 **Kaywana blood.**
Edgar Mittelholzer. London: Secker & Warburg, 1958. 523p.

The final volume of the *Kaywana Trilogy* again emphasizes the working out of the sexual urge through the story of Dirk van Groenwegel. Mittelholzer achieves a vivid and disturbing portrait, blending history and romance.

532 **My bones and my flute; a ghost story in the old-fashioned manner.**
Edgar Mittelholzer. London: Secker & Warburg, 1955. 222p.

Influenced by the stories of M. R. James, this tale of the supernatural, set in Guyana, has been called one of the best ghost stories in the English language. It is also one of Mittelholzer's more positive efforts, a story in which human courage successfully combats the powers of diabolic evil.

533 **A swarthy boy.**
Edgar Mittelholzer. London: Putnam, 1963. 157p.

Mittelholzer's autobiography emphasizes his formative years in Guyana.

534 **A morning at the office, a novel.**
Edgar Mittelholzer. London: Heinemann, 1974. 256p. (Caribbean Writers Series, no. 11).

Mittelholzer uses an office in Trinidad during a single morning as a mcirocosm in which to observe the interplay between race, sex and class relations in the West Indies.

James Rodway

535 **In Guiana wilds; a study of two women.**
James Rodway. Boston, Massachusetts: L. C. Page, 1899. 270p.

Rodway's tale of Amerindians and English missionaries has been called the first distinctively Guyanese novel.

A. J. Seymour

536 **Selected poems.**
A. J. Seymour. Lithographic, 1965. 95p.

A booklet of approximately fifty poems chosen from Seymour's work.

Eric Walrond

537 **Tropic death.**

Eric Walrond. New York: Boni & Liveright, 1926. 282p.

This book of ten short stories won critical acclaim when it was published in 1926. Walrond's tales, set in Guyana, Barbados, and Panama, draw upon Caribbean folklore for inspiration, blending realism with the supernatural.

A. R. F. Webber

538 **Those that be in bondage: a tale of East Indian indentures and sunlit western waters.**

A. R. F. Webber. Georgetown: Daily Chronicle, 1917. 236p.

A novel that exposes the evils of the indenture system through the symbolism of an inter-racial marriage between a white plantation overseer and a beautiful East Indian immigrant girl.

Denis Williams

539 **Other leopards.**

Denis Williams, with an introduction by Edward Baugh. London: Heinemann, 1983. 221p. (Caribbean Writers Series, no. 22).

Originally published in 1963, Williams's first novel examines the West Indians' response to Africa through the experiences of its protagonist, a British-educated Guyanese who goes to the Sudan. Although perhaps better known as a painter and archaeologist than as a writer, Williams has also written short stories and published one other novel, *The third temptation* (London: Calder & Boyars, 1968).

Criticism of individual writers

Martin Carter

540 **Resistance poems: the voice of Martin Carer.**

Edward Kamau Brathwaite. *Caribbean Quarterly*, vol. 23, nos. 2 & 3 (June–Sept. 1977), p. 7-23.

A survey of the work of the Guyanese poet covering the period from his first published work in 1951 to his writings of the 1970s.

Wilson Harris

541 **Wilson Harris and the modern tradition: a new architecture of the world.**
Sandra E. Drake. Westport, Connecticut: Greenwood, 1986. 213p. bibliog. maps. (Contributions in Afro-American and African Studies, no. 93).

A scholarly critical study of Harris's fiction, concentrating on four of his novels: *Palace of the peacock* (1960) (q.v.), *Tumatumari* (1968), *Ascent to Omai* (1970), and *Genesis of the clowns* (1977). Drake's aim is to clarify how Harris's writing, 'constitutes part of the modern tradition, from the perspective of the Third World'. The volume includes a bibliographic essay commenting on primary and secondary sources. It is also illustrated with several maps and diagrams that should prove useful to Harris's readers.

542 **Wilson Harris.**
Hena Maes-Jelinek. Boston, Massachusetts: Twayne, 1982. 191p. bibliog. (Twayne's World Authors Series).

A compact critical study that interprets seventeen of Harris's fictional works, both novels and short stories. The selected bibliography lists primary and secondary sources.

543 **Wilson Harris: a bibliography.**
Michael J. Abaray. *Bulletin of Bibliography*, vol. 38, no. 4 (Oct.–Dec. 1981), p. 189-93.

This presents an unannotated catalogue of primary and secondary sources. Intended to supplement the primary sources listed in McDowell's *Bibliography of literature from Guyana* (q.v.), Abaray's work covers Harris's own writings since 1975. His listing of secondary material aims to be exhaustive and includes book reviews and interviews as well as criticism.

544 **The naked design; a reading of *Palace of the peacock*.**
Hena Maes-Jelinek. Aarhus, Denmark: Dangaroo, 1976. 64p.

This makes a close study of the imagery of Harris's 1960 novel, *Palace of the peacock* (q.v.), the opening movement of the *Guyana quarter* (q.v.).

545 **Wilson Harris and the Caribbean novel.**
Michael Gilkes. London: Longman; Trinidad: Longman Caribbean, 1975. 159p. bibliog.

In one of the few book-length studies of Harris's work, Gilkes brings Jungian psychological theory to bear on Harris's fiction, discussing his novels up to *Black Marsden* (1972).

546 **Kas-Kas: interviews with three Caribbean writers in Texas: George Lamming, C. L. R. James, Wilson Harris.**
Edited by Ian Munro, Reinhard Sander. Austin, Texas: African and Afro-American Research Institute of the University of Texas, 1972. p. 43-56. bibliog.

Of interest in this volume is 'Interview with Wilson Harris'. Harris was interviewed by the editors of this volume in 1972 at the University of Texas at Austin, where he spent a semester as Visiting Professor of Ethnic Studies and English. Harris answers questions about his own work and comments on the work of other Caribbean authors.

547 ***Tumatumari* and the imagination of Wilson Harris.**
Joyce Alder. *Journal of Commonwealth Literature*, no. 7 (July 1969), p. 20-31.

A discussion of Harris's eighth novel, *Tumatumari*, comparing its complexity to his relatively straightforward work, *The waiting room.*

548 **Wilson Harris; a philosophical approach.**
C. L. R. James. St. Augustine, Trinidad: University of the West Indies, 1965. 15p. (General Public Lecture Series. West Indian Literature, no. 1).

Triniadian intellectual C. L. R. James approaches Harris's fiction through Martin Heidegger's existentialism.

Edgar Mittelholzer

549 **Edgar Mittelholzer's tragic vision.**
William J. Howard. *Caribbean Quarterly*, vol. 16, no. 4 (Dec. 1970), p. 19-28.

A brief article that is largely an analysis of Mittelholzer's *A morning at the office*, which Howard sees as, thematically, the key to Mittelholzer's work. In his view, the book contains, 'the two major melodies which counterpointed [Mittelholzer's] entire career', these being a situation beyond the control of a character in which longing encounters frustration and the importance of psychic phenomena.

550 **Edgar Mittelholzer: moralist or pornographer?**
F. M. Birbalsingh. *Journal of Commonwealth Literature*, no. 7 (July 1969), p. 88-103.

Birbalsingh compares Mittelholzer with the early-nineteenth-century American novelist, Charles Brockden Brown, and finds in Mittelholzer's work a, 'pattern of moral purpose subverted by sensation (mainly eroticism)'.

551 **Edgar Mittelholzer: the man and his work.**
A. J. Seymour. Georgetown: Ministry of Education, 1968. 53p. (Edgar Mittelholzer Memorial Lectures, 1967).

A summary of Mittelholzer's life and work, which centres on the idea that 'when (Mittelholzer) could no longer master the forces acting on his own life, he applied the principle so often expressed in his novels of victory or death . . .'.

Foreign fiction set in Guyana

552 **Man on a rope.**
George Harmon Coxe. New York: Knopf, 1956. 213p.

A mystery novel set in Guyana, the plot of which revolves around the black market in diamonds. Coxe, an American, was one of the few detective-story writers to utilize Guyana as a backdrop for fictional crime. *Man on a rope* is the second of his books set in the country. In an earlier novel, *Assignment in Guiana*, (New York: Knopf, 1942), Guyana was the scene of international wartime intrigue.

553 **The lost world; being an account of the recent amazing adventures of Professor Challenger, Lord John Roxton, Professor Summerlee and Mr. E. D. Malone of the 'Daily Gazette'.**
Sir Arthur Conan Doyle. London: Hodder & Stoughton, 1912. 319p.

An adventure novel in which Professor Challenger leads an expedition into the South American jungle and finds a 'lost world' of prehistoric animals preserved on the top of a table mountain. The novel drew its inspiration from speculation stimulated by Guyana's Mount Roraima, a steep-sided plateau mountain discovered in the tropical rain forest.

554 **Green mansions; a romance of the tropical forest.**
William Henry Hudson. London; Toronto: J. M. Dent; New York: E. P. Dutton, 1923. 323p. (Collected Works of W. H. Hudson). Reprinted, New York: AMS.

Originally published in 1904, Hudson's novel is a fantasy set in the southern forest of Guyana. Rima, a strange, beautiful bird-girl, haunts the forest, warbling a musical language that no one understands. When a search for her origins fails, she dies.

Libraries, Archives and Museums

Within Guyana

555 **Guyana.**
In: *World guide to libraries; Internationales bibliotheks-handbuch.* New York; London; Paris: K. G. Saur, 1986, 7th ed. p. 340-41. (Handbook of International Documentation and Information, vol. 8).

Offers brief directory information on Guyana's National Library, university and college libraries and special and public libraries. Provides the name, address, year of foundation, current director and size of collection for each library.

556 **Research guide to Central America and the Caribbean.**
Editor-in-chief Kenneth Grieb, associate editors, Ralph Lee Woodward, Jr., Graeme S. Mount, Thomas G. Mathews. Madison, Wisconsin: University of Wisconsin Press, 1985. 431p.

An up-to-date and useful reference tool that identifies archival resources available to researchers in the Caribbean area. A description of archival and other record depositories in Guyana by Mary Noel Menezes can be found on pages 360-63: the Berbice Legal Registry, the Caribbean Research Library, the University of Guyana at Turkeyen, the National Archives and various other depositories are covered. The volume also contains several review-bibliographical essays of particular interest to Guyanists: 'Exploitative Systems; Slavery, Commerce, and Industry' (Richard B. Sheridan); 'Migrant Groups in the Caribbean' (Marianne D. Ramesar); 'An Appraisal of Caribbean Scholarship' (Gordon K. Lewis) and 'East Indians in the West Indies' (Brinsley Samaroo). Other references to Guyana can be located through the volume's index. Basic information is provided for each institution listed, including the scope of its holdings, unique aspects or restrictions, availability, hours of operation and prevailing conditions.

557 **A handbook of Latin American and Caribbean national archives/Guia de los archivos nacionales de America Latina y el Caribe.**

Ann K. Nauman. Detroit: Blaine Ethridge, 1983. p. 27 & 89. bibliog.

A first-time user's dirctory that provides information on materials, services, requirements and restrictions for each Latin American/Caribbean country's national archives. Data on the National Archives of Guyana, Georgetown, is given in English on page twenty-seven and in Spanish on page eighty-nine. Nauman comments that a knowledge of Dutch is necessary for those wishing to conduct research in Guyana's eighteenth-century archival materials.

558 **Guyana, libraries in.**

Thomas Kabdebo. In: *Encyclopedia of library and information science.* Edited by Allen Kent (et al). New York; Basel, Switzerland: Marcel Dekker, 1981, vol. 10, p. 248-49. bibliog.

Provides information on Guyana's libraries as of 1981 and describes the Public Free Library in Georgetown, the University of Guyana Library, the Guyana Medical Science Library, the Guyana Society Library, the John F. Kennedy Library of USIS and the British Council Library.

559 **The University of Guyana Library: past, present, and future.**

Thomas Kabdebo, Yvonne Stephenson. *Library Association Record*, vol. 72, no. 7 (July 1970), p. 258-60.

Located on the University campus at Turkeyen, the University of Guyana Library was founded in 1963. In this article, two Guyanese librarians discuss its current status and plans for development.

560 **Report on the archives of British Guiana.**

Clinton V. Black. Georgetown: Daily Chronicle, 1955. 23p.

A government-sponsored survey of Guyana's archival depositories which was conducted by a Jamaican archivist.

561 **British Guiana Museum; centenary history and guide, 1853-1953.**

Vincent Roth. Georgetown: Daily Chronicle, 1953. 105p.

Now the Guyana Museum, the British Guiana Museum was founded in 1853 by the Royal Agricultural and Commercial Society. Its collections cover Guyanese industry, art, history, anthropology and zoology. This guidebook and history was compiled by the museum's curator.

562 **Guide to libraries and archives in Central America and the West Indies, Panama, Bermuda, and British Guiana, supplemented with information on private libraries, bookbinding, book selling and printing.**
Arthur E. Gropp. New Orleans: Middle American Research Institute, Tulane University of Louisiana, 1941. p. 213-32. map. bibliog. Middle American Research Series. Publication 10).

Although out-dated in the information it provides on practical details of hours and services, this reference work can still be profitably consulted by researchers seeking library materials. The section on British Guiana surveys the collections of public and private libraries and archival repositories in the country, and lists representative titles held by various institutions.

563 **Records of Barbados, Demerara, and the Leeward Islands.**
In: *Caribbeana: being miscellaneous papers relating to the history, genealogy, topography, and antiquities of the British West Indies.* Edited by Vere Langford Oliver. London: Mitchell Hughes & Clarke, 1914, p. 358-62.

Includes a short but detailed note based on Oliver's visit to the Georgetown Public Record Office in 1913 and 1914. Mention is made of 140 volumes of Dutch deeds and other volumes covering transports, mortgages, wills, etc. that he viewed there. A very early review of archival materials in Guyana was published by the Guyanese antiquarian and bibliophile Nicholas Darnell Davis, *The records of British Guiana*, (Demerara, n.p., 1888).

Periodical

564 **Guyana Library Association Bulletin.**
Georgetown, 1970- . semi-annual.

This work is indexed in *Library and Information Abstracts*. It has a circulation of one hundred.

Outside Guyana

565 **The catalogue of the West India Reference Library.**
Institute of Jamaica, Kingston, West India Reference Library. Millwood, New York: Kraus International, 1980. 2 vols. in 6.

This catalogue of the collection of what is now the National Library of Jamaica constitutes a retrospective bibliography of the entire Caribbean area. It lists many items pertaining to Guyana.

566 **A guide to manuscript sources for the history of Latin America and the Caribbean in the British Isles.**
Peter Walne. Foreword by R. A. Humphreys. London: Oxford University Press for the Institute of Latin American Studies, 1973. 580p.

This comprehensive listing of repositories in the United Kingdom is the basic reference source for those seeking archival materials on Guyanese history. Collections of manuscripts, private and public papers and the archives of business firms are described.

567 **Directory of libraries and special collections on Latin America and the West Indies.**
Bernard Naylor, Laurence Hallewell, Colin Steele. London: Athone, for the Institute of Latin American Studies, 1975. 161p. (Institute of Latin American Studies. Monograph no. 5).

Represents an up-to-date source for the location of Caribbean area materials in Great Britain.

568 **Guide to resources for Commonwealth studies in London, Oxford and Cambridge, with bibliographical and other information.**
A. R. Hewitt. London: Athlone, for the Institute of Commonwealth Studies, University of London, 1957. 219p. bibliog.

This excellent work lists institutional and library resources for the study of the Commonwealth – mainly in the areas of history and the social sciences – to be found in London, Oxford, and Cambridge.

569 **Subject catalogue of the library of the Royal Empire Society.**
Evans Lewin. London: Royal Empire Society, 1932. 4 vols. Reprinted, with a new introduction by Donald H. Simpson. London: Dawsons, for the Royal Commonwealth Society, 1967.

A comprehensive bibliography of the Empire-Commonwealth up to 1930, with carefully catalogued listings of periodical articles and government papers as well as books.

570 **Subject catalogue of the Royal Commonwealth Society.**
Royal Commonwealth Society, Library. Boston: G. K. Hall, 1971. vols. 5 & 7.

Continues the bibliography of the countries of the Commonwealth that began with the *Subject catalogue of the library of the Royal Empire Society* (q.v.). The volumes containing materials for the study of Guyana are entitled *The Americas* and *Biography, voyages, and travels, World War I and World War II.* A two-volume first supplement to this catalogue has also been published (Boston: G. K. Hall, 1977).

Mass Media

General

571 **Caribbean mass communications; a comprehensive bibliography.**
John A. Lent. Waltham, Massachusetts: Crossroads, African Studies Association, 1981. p. 34-40. (Archival and Bibliographic Series).

Represents a useful reference tool. The Guyana section lists bibliographical references to books, periodical articles and newspaper articles on the country's mass communications, advertising, broadcasting, film, freedom of the press, history of the press and print media. The majority of the entries are unannotated.

572 **Mass media in national development: governmental perspectives in Jamaica and Guyana.**
Marlene Cuthbert. *Caribbean Quarterly*, vol. 23, no. 4 (Dec. 1977), p. 90-105.

'This paper examines the struggles of two developing Caribbean nations, as they attempt to define the role of the media in their national development.' After a general overview, the author devotes separate sections to Jamaica and Guyana, pointing out that Guyana has adopted a planned approach which has been implemented by government take-over of the press and other available media and by government control of newsprint and printing equipment. The government has also banned 'bad' films. In Guyana, the question is not press freedom but whether the press is playing a positive role – as defined by the government – in national development.

573 **Ethnic images in Guyanese advertising.**
Yvonne J. Bickerton. *Caribbean Studies*, vol. 11, no. 2 (July 1971), p. 90-97.

Bickerton analyses the results for Guyana of a three-month 1969 study of ethnic images appearing in newspaper advertisements in Jamaica, Barbados, Trinidad, and Guyana. According to the data collected, European ethnic images are dominant in Guyanese advertising.

Broadcasting

574 **Broadcasting in Guyana.**
Ron Sanders. London; Boston, Massachusetts: Routledge & Kegan Paul, 1978. 77p. maps. bibliog. (Case Studies on Broadcasting Systems, no. 6).

One of a series of International Institute of Communications case studies on broadcasting in countries of the Third World, this book presents a summary of the current state of radio communications in Guyana.

Printing and publishing

575 **Early printing and the book trade in the West Indies.**
Roderick Cave. *Library Quarterly*, vol. 48, no. 2 (April 1978), p. 163-92. bibliog.

An article that covers developments in printing prior to 1865 in British and British-influenced Caribbean territories. Cave details the establishment of presses in the region and notes the prevalence of journalism over literary production. In his view it was, 'the decline of the planter class and the weakening of the sugar colonies' economic position [that] prevented indigenous publishing from developing successfully'. While there is little that is directly concerned with Guyanese printing, the article is of interest to students for its overview of the early West Indian publishing situation within which Guyanese publishing took place.

576 **Educational publishing and book production in the English-speaking Caribbean.**
Alvona Alleyne, Pam Mordecai. *Library Trends*, vol. 26, no. 4 (spring 1978), p. 575-89. bibliog.

The authors survey the region's educational publishing at all levels – primary, secondary, and tertiary – concentrating mainly on Guyana, Jamaica, and Trinidad. The article also furnishes informative facts on the Caribbean's periodical press.

577 **The press in British Guiana.**
James Rodway. *Proceedings of the American Antiquarian Society*, vol. 28, pt. 2 (Oct. 16, 1918), p. 274-90. bibliog.

An informative and detailed history of printing and early printers in Guyana from 1793, when an 'advertentie blad' – probably called the *Essequebo en Demerara Courant* – was published by J. C. de la Coste, up to 1820. Rodway discusses the printing and publishing of advertising sheets, newspapers, almanacs and books in the colony under both Dutch and British rule, and includes a valuable 'List of British Guiana Newspapers Before 1820'. This article was also issued as a separate pamphlet (Worcester, Massachusetts: American Antiquarian Society, 1918). A more recent publication on Guyana's newspapers is Mona Telesford's, 'Notes on Guyanese newspapers', which appeared in *Working papers on West Indian printing* (Mona, Jamaica: Dept. of Library Studies, University of the West Indies, series 2, 1976).

Newspapers

578 **Guyana Chronicle.**

Georgetown, 1881- . daily.

Guyana's only daily newspaper, which has been state-owned since 1971. In 1973, the government bought the paper's competitor, the *Guyana Graphic* – at that time the country's leading daily – and merged the two papers. The *Chronicle* reports the government line with little criticism. It appears six days a week and has a circulation of 61,000. Its Sunday edition, the *Sunday Chronicle*, has a circulation of 102,000.

579 **New Nation.**

Georgetown, 1955- . weekly.

This is the newspaper of Guyana's ruling party, the People's National Congress. It has a circulation of 26,000.

580 **The Catholic Standard.**

Georgetown, 1905- . weekly.

An opposition newspaper, published by the Roman Catholic Church, *Catholic Standard* has had difficulties with the Guyanese government. It was sued for libel by government officials in August, 1982, and the government has refused to allow it to accept donated newsprint from overseas. The newspaper has a circulation of 10,000.

581 **Mirror.**

Edited by Janet Jagan. Georgetown, 1963- . weekly.

A Sunday paper, which is the organ of the People's Progressive Party. Its publication was suspended for some time because of newsprint supply problems caused by the government. Its circulation numbers 20,000.

Newspapers

582 **Stabroek News.**

Edited by Cecil Griffith. Georgetown, 1986- . weekly.

This is Guyana's newest paper, an independent with a circulation of 15,000.

Reference Works

583 **Guyana.**

In: *World of learning*, 1988. London: Europa, 38th ed. p. 595-96.

Provides annually updated directory information on learned societies, research institutes, libraries, museums, colleges and the University of Guyana. Entries list names, addresses, directors, principal personnel and publications.

584 **Caribbean business directory, 1987/88.**

Grand Cayman, Cayman Islands, British West Indies: Caribbean Publishing Company, 1987. 608p. map.

This business directory for the Caribbean region includes Guyana. It is organized in two sections: white pages provide company listing by country; yellow pages are divided into 600 alphabetical product categories, from abrasive materials to zoos. Names, addresses and telephone numbers are also given.

585 **Personalities Caribbean; the international guide to who's who in the West Indies, Bahamas, Bermuda.**

Edited by Anthony Lancelot Levy, Hedley Powell Jacobs. Kingston, Jamaica: Personalities, 1983. 1027p. 7th ed.

Offers standard biographical information on notable living persons, some entries being accompanied by photographs. The guide is revised every two years. The Guyana section is on pages 175-209; 'General Listings' sections include Guyanese living abroad.

586 **Caribbean writers; a bio-bibliographical-critical encyclopedia.**
Edited by Donald E. Herdeck, Maurice A. Lubin, John Figueroa, Dorothy A. Figueroa, José Alcantara, Margaret L. Herdeck. Washington, DC: Three Continents, 1979. 943p. bibliog.

A fundamental reference work on Caribbean literature that pulls together much material that would be difficult to locate. Each writer receives a capsule biography followed by a bibliography that lists both the subject's own work and critical studies. Language groups are dealt with separately. The Anglophone literature section includes an 'Essay on West Indian Writing' that discusses the literature of the English-Speaking Caribbean and provides a country-by-country listing of writers from the formerly-British West Indies. The volume also contains seven excellent bibliographies on the Anglophone Caribbean, entitled: 'West Indian Literature and Culture: Bibliographies'; 'The West Indies: Critical Studies'; 'West Indian Literature: General Anthologies and Collections'; 'Literature Pre-1900'; 'Background Books (Selected)'; 'Historical Writings Pre-1900'; 'Background Books (Selected)'; 'General Background Studies on Various Islands Post-1900 and West Indian Literature: Selected Journals'.

587 **Historical dictionary of the British Caribbean.**
William Lux. Metuchen, New Jersey: Scarecrow, 1975. p. 87-118. bibliog. (Latin American Historical Dictionaries, no. 12).

Offers short definitions of historical, social, economic and geographic terms pertaining to Guyana, arranged alphabetically, from 'Abolition' to 'Wismar'. Also includes a useful list of the British governors of the colony, from 1831 to independence.

Bibliographies

Current

588 **Bibliography of the English-Speaking Caribbean: Books, Articles, and Reviews in English from the Arts, Humanities, and Social Sciences.**
Edited by Robert J. Neymeyer. Parkersburgh, Iowa: The Author, 1979- . semi-annual.

A serial subject bibliography that lists publications on the Anglophone Caribbean that have appeared in North America, Europe, and the Caribbean region.

589 **The CARICOM Bibliography.**
Georgetown: Library of the Secretariat of the Caribbean Community, 1977- . annual.

Guyanese books and the first issues of periodicals published in Guyana appear in this yearly listing of materials pubished in Caribbean Community (CARICOM) member territories. Entries for Guyana are drawn from the *Guyanese National Bibliography* (q.v.). Arrangement is in two sections, author/title and classified subject.

590 **Guyanese National Bibliography; a Subject List of New Books Printed in the Republic of Guyana, Based on the Books Deposited at the National Library.**
Georgetown: National Library, 1973- . quarterly.

Published by the National Library in Georgetown, the legal repository for material printed in Guyana. The main listing is by Dewey Decimal Classification, with author, title and subject indexes. Excludes brief pamphlets and certain government documents.

591 **Caribbean Studies.**
Rio Piedras, Puerto Rico: Institute of Caribbean Studies, University of Puerto Rico, 1961- . quarterly.

The 'Current bibliography' section in each issue of this scholarly journal is a 'selected compilation of current books, periodical literature and certain documentary material of interest to Caribbeanists'.

592 **Handbook of Latin American studies.**
Edited by Dolores Moyano Martin (et al). Cambridge, Massachusetts: Harvard University Press, 1936-51. Gainesville: University of Florida Press, 1952-79. Austin, Texas; London: Univeristy of Texas Press, 1980- .

The *Handbook of Latin American studies* (HLAS) is the basic source for current Latin American bibliography, including the Anglophone countries of the Caribbean region. Since 1965, the work has been published in two volumes appearing in alternate years, one volume covering the social sciences and its companion the humanities. Entries are annotated by scholars with reviews of subject literature often provided by authorities. Books, periodical articles, pamphlets and conference papers in all major languages are included (with annotations in English or Spanish). A cumulative author index to the first thirty years of the publication has been compiled by Francisco José Cardona and Maria Elena Cardona (*Author index to Handbook of Latin American studies, nos. 1-28, 1936-1966*, Gainesville: University of Florida, 1968).

Retrospective

593 **The English-speaking Caribbean: a bibliography of bibliographies.**
Alma Jordan, Barbara Comissiong. Boston, Massachusetts: G. K. Hall, 1984. 436p. (Reference Publication in Latin American Studies).

An important reference tool consisting of annotated entries listing both published and unpublished bibliographies on all aspects of the Anglophone Caribbean. The main arrangement is by broad subject classification, with form and country subdivisions. Bibliographical materials on Guyana are easily located either directly or through the index. 'The work includes both brief and substantial bibliographies whether unpublished, privately issued, appearing in conference proceedings, or otherwise published as separate items. It also includes lists appearing in journals . . . Bibliographies provided in books were included only where [they were] considered . . . significant.'

594 **Latin America and the Caribbean II: a dissertation bibliography.**
Marian C. Walters. Ann Arbor, Michigan: University Microfilms International, 1980. 78p.

Supplements and updates Carl W. Deal's bibliography (q.v.) and follows the organization of the earlier volume.

595 **Bibliography of the Mazaruni area, Guyana.**
A. Fournier. Edited by J. Benjamin. Georgetown: Upper Mazaruni Development Authority, 1978. 188p.

A general bibliography listing approximately 1,300 citations to works pertaining to the Mazaruni district in the Guyanese interior. Covers a variety of subjects – history, geology, Amerindian tribes and so on – and includes unpublished as well as published items. Materials in languages other than English are listed.

596 **Latin America and the Caribbean; a dissertation bibliography.**
Carl W. Deal. Ann Arbor, Michigan: University Microfilms International, 1978. 164p.

This is available gratis from the publisher, and lists more than 7,200 theses through to 1977 that are available from University Microfilms. Entries have a subject arrangement and author index.

597 **The complete Caribbeana, 1900-1975; a bibliographic guide to the scholarly literature.**
Lambros Comitas. Millwood, New York: KTO Press, 1977. 4 vols.

The major retrospective source for non-Hispanic Caribbean bibliography, this publication is an expansion of Comitas's, *Caribbeana, 1900-1965* (Seattle: University of Washington Press for the Research Institute for the Study of Man, 1968). The work is organized in four volumes: Vol. 1: *People*; Vol. 2: *Institutions*; Vol. 3: *Resources* and Vol. 4: *Indexes*. The plan of the work is topical. There are nine major thematic sections and sixty-three topical chapters. The work contains 17,000 citations to all types of printed materials on, 'those mainland and insular possessions or former possessions of Great Britain, France, and Netherlands, and the United States in the Caribbean region.' Guyana is included. Each bibliographic citation gives the location of the item, but there are no annotations. Volumes are indexed by author, subject and geographical location.

598 **Caribbean studies, part I.**
Edith F. Hurwitz. *Choice*, vol. 12, no. 4 (June 1975), p. 487-502. bibliog.

A narrative bibliographical essay with an appended 'Works Cited' list that is for the most part a selection of books in history and the social sciences. This part covers general studies of the Caribbean region and materials on the Commonwealth Caribbean.

599 **Caribbean studies, part II.**
Edith F. Hurwitz. *Choice*, vol. 12, nos. 5-6 (July/Aug. 1975), p. 639-47. bibliog.

The 'Guyana' section, p. 643-44, consists of several paragraphs of narrative discussion and a list of twelve books.

600 **Theses on the Commonwealth Caribbean, 1891-1973.**
Commonwealth Caribbean Resource Centre. London, Ontario: Office of International Education, University of Western Ontario, 1974. 136p.

This covers dissertations accepted in universities of Great Britain, the United States and Canada. There is an author listing and a geographical index.

601 **Theses on Caribbean topics 1778-1968.**
Enid M. Baa. San Juan, Puerto Rico: Institute of Caribbean Studies and the University of Puerto Rico, 1970. 146p. bibliog. (Caribbean Bibliographic Series, no. 1).

The main body of the work is a list of doctoral dissertations, arranged alphabetically by author, to which is added a similar listing of Masters and other theses. Four indexes allow the user to locate items by the university at which the dissertation was written; the country studied in the dissertation and the year that the dissertation was written. Coverage is most complete for theses submitted to universities in the United States, England and France.

602 **Latin America and the Caribbean; a bibliographical guide to works in English.**
S. A. Bayitch. Coral Gables, Florida: University of Miami Press; Dobbs Ferry, New York: Oceana, 1967. 943p. (University of Miami School of Law: Interamerican Legal Studies, vol. 10).

This older, retrospective, social science oriented bibliography is probably most useful to students of Guyana for its legal references. Statutes, ordinances and court reports are listed, as well as references to texts of Guyanese Constitutions, 1831 to 1966. Items pertaining to Guyana can be found in sections on the Caribbean (p. 265-289), the British West Indies (p. 803-865), and Guyana (p. 835-843). The brief, unannotated entries list books, periodical articles and government reports.

603 **A bibliography of neo-African literature from Africa, America and the Caribbean.**
Janheinz Jahn. London: André Deutsch, 1965. 359p.

This bibliography of 'the new literature of African culture' is an unannotated listing of the creative literary work of individual authors, including plays, essays, anthologies and translations into foreign languages. Guyanese writers listed include: E. R. Braithwaite, Jan Carew, Martin Carter, Oscar Ronald Dathorne, Wilson Harris, Lauchmonen, Wordsworth Albert McAndrew, Edgar Mittelholzer, Ivan van Sertima and Arthur J. Seymour.

604 **A selective guide to the English literature on the Netherlands West Indies; with a supplement on British Guiana.**

Philip Hanson Hiss. New York: Netherlands Information Bureau, 1943. 129p. (Booklets of the Netherlands Information Bureau, no. 9).

Hiss explains in his preface to this volume that, 'The supplement on British Guiana has been included . . . because Demerara, Berbice, and Essequebo, the British Guiana of today, were first colonized by the Dutch and were not finally ceded to Great Britain until the London Convention of August 13, 1814; [and] because experience in British Guiana in many respects parallels that of Suriname and partially compensates for certain deficiencies in the English literature of the latter country'. The British Guiana supplement, p. 114-24, is an unannotated, classified listing of books, periodical articles and government publications in the following categories: general works, history, missions, politics, law, social conditions, economy, anthropology, geography, science and languages and literature. Only English language works are included.

605 **A bibliography of the negro in Africa and America.**

Monroe N. Work. New York: H. W. Wilson, 1928. 698p. Reprinted, New York, Octagon, 1970.

In this bibliography the section on the West Indies contains references to works about the Afro-Guyanese. Of special interest is the section, 'A bibliography of bibliographies on the West Indies', p. 655-658, which lists published and unpublished bibliographies of archival materials, manuscripts, book trade catalogues, and library catalogues. International in scope, this list should be quite valuable to researchers.

606 **Bibliography of the West Indies (excluding Jamaica).**

Frank Cundall. Kingston, Jamaica: Institute of Jamaica, 1909. 179p. Reprinted, New York; London: Johnson Reprint, 1971.

A pioneer effort in Caribbean bibliography by a librarian at the Institute of Jamaica, this work is based on the collection at the Institute as of 1909. Items not in the Institute's Library are asterisked. The bibliography follows a chronological arrangement under geographical divisions, with five additional sections dealing with general topics: West Indies Generally; Slavery; Buccaneers; British West Africa and Parliamentary Papers relating to the West Indies Generally. The last category lists Parliamentary Papers from 1750 to 1900. Books, pamphlets and government reports are listed with abbreviated titles and no annotations. The bibliography is indexed by authors, subjects of memoirs and cartographers.

Indexes

There follow three separate indexes: authors (personal and corporate); titles; and subjects. Title entries are italicized and refer either to the main titles (books), or to other works cited in the annotations. The numbers refer to bibliographic entry rather than page numbers. Individual index entries are arranged in alphabetical sequence.

Index of Authors

G

H

I

J

Index of Titles

H

I

Q

R

S

T

U

V

W

Z

Index of Subjects

B

C

G

N

Q

R

T

U

Map of Guyana

This map shows the more important towns and other features.

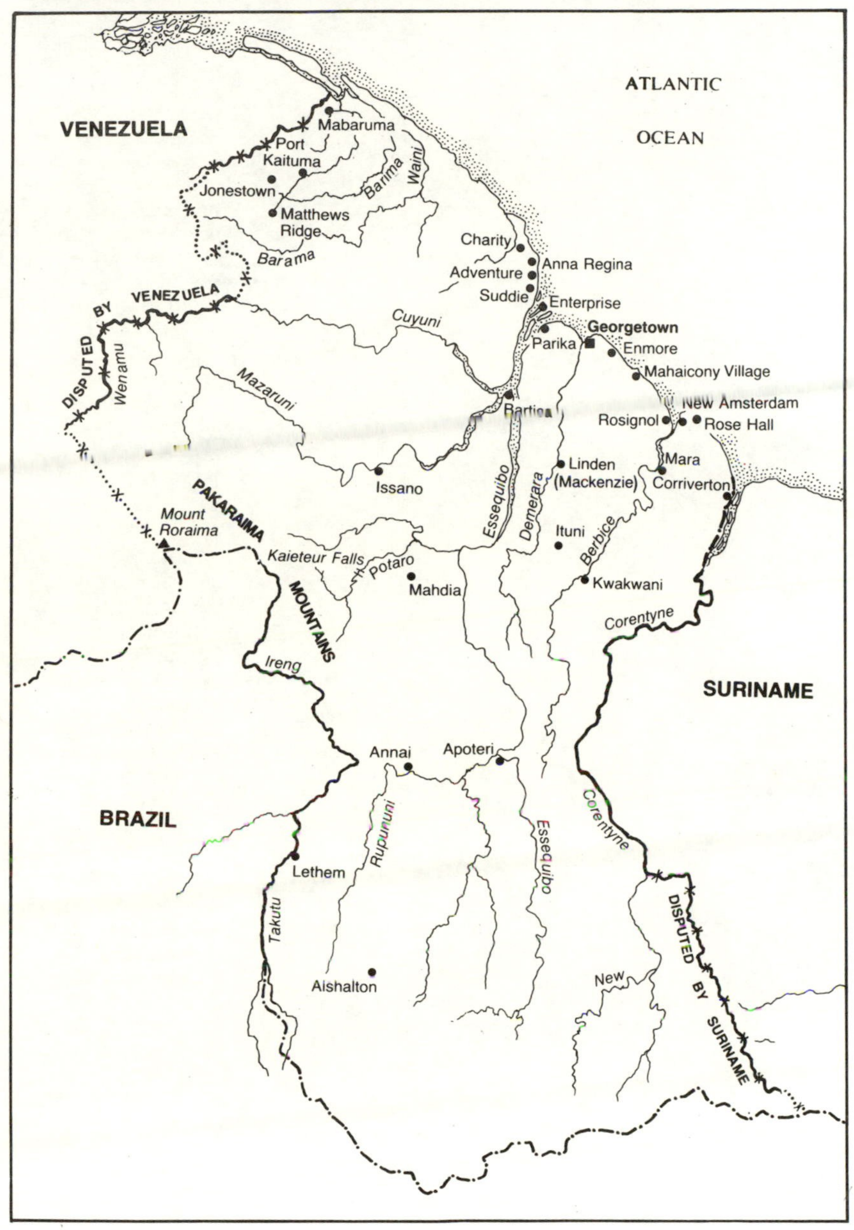